Our world today

Derek Heater

Oxford University Press

Oxford University Press, Walton Street, Oxford OX2 6DP

Oxford London
New York Toronto Melbourne Auckland
Kuala Lumpur Singapore Hong Kong Tokyo
Delhi Bombay Calcutta Madras Karachi
Nairobi Dar es Salaam Cape Town

and associated companies in
Beirut Berlin Ibadan Mexico City Nicosia

Oxford is a trade mark of Oxford University Press

© Oxford University Press 1985
First published 1985
ISBN 0 19 9132941

Set by Eta Services, Beccles, Suffolk
Printed in Great Britain by Butler & Tanner Ltd, Frome

Preface

This book has been written to serve as a companion to *Our World This Century* – an introductory twentieth-century world history.

On the one hand an understanding of the contemporary world really needs an historical perspective, the approach used in *Our World This Century*. And yet, on the other hand, some crucially important facets of the present day world are best studied through themes presented from the perspective of the present, unrelated to the framework of chronological narrative. Ten such themes are analysed in this book.

Again, every effort has been made to keep the language as simple and the design as attractive as possible. It is much easier to write historical narrative than contemporary analysis in simple language. I trust, however, that the present book is reasonably comprehensible to those readers approaching this kind of study for the first time. It will have served its purpose if it stimulates the reader to a greater interest in the news as presented by the media and assists in the understanding of current events as they occur.

Derek Heater

Contents

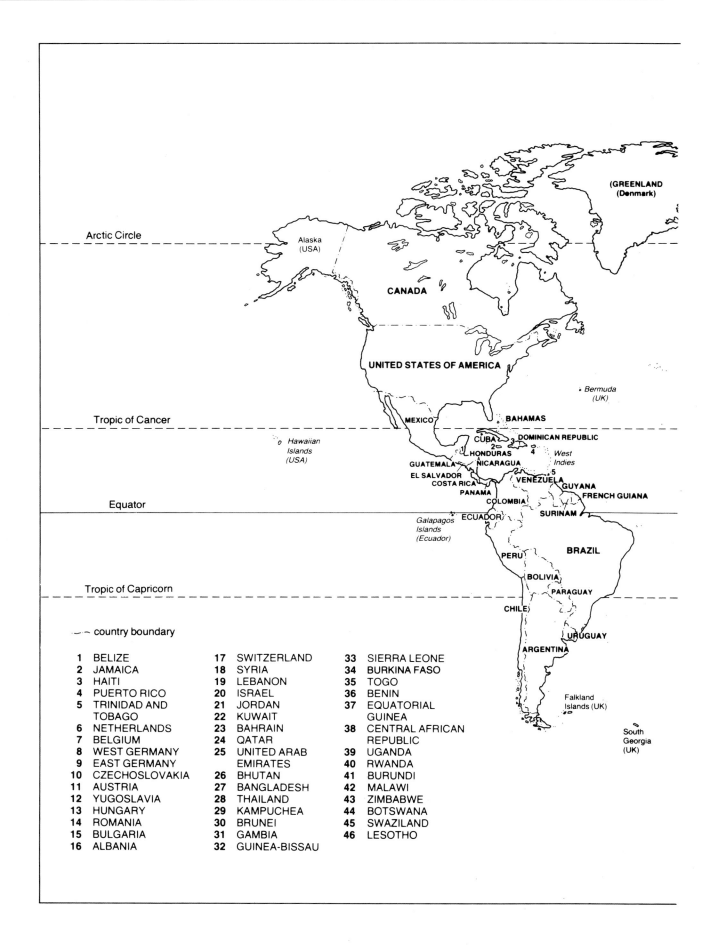

Arctic Circle

(GREENLAND
(Denmark)

Alaska
(USA)

CANADA

UNITED STATES OF AMERICA

Bermuda
(UK)

Tropic of Cancer

MEXICO

BAHAMAS

Hawaiian
Islands
(USA)

CUBA 3 DOMINICAN REPUBLIC
2 4
HONDURAS West
Indies
GUATEMALA NICARAGUA 5
EL SALVADOR VENEZUELA GUYANA
COSTA RICA FRENCH GUIANA
PANAMA
COLOMBIA SURINAM

Equator

Galapagos
Islands
(Ecuador)

ECUADOR

PERU

BRAZIL

BOLIVIA

Tropic of Capricorn

PARAGUAY

CHILE

URUGUAY

ARGENTINA

Falkland
Islands (UK)

South
Georgia
(UK)

--- country boundary

1	BELIZE	**17**	SWITZERLAND
2	JAMAICA	**18**	SYRIA
3	HAITI	**19**	LEBANON
4	PUERTO RICO	**20**	ISRAEL
5	TRINIDAD AND	**21**	JORDAN
	TOBAGO	**22**	KUWAIT
6	NETHERLANDS	**23**	BAHRAIN
7	BELGIUM	**24**	QATAR
8	WEST GERMANY	**25**	UNITED ARAB
9	EAST GERMANY		EMIRATES
10	CZECHOSLOVAKIA	**26**	BHUTAN
11	AUSTRIA	**27**	BANGLADESH
12	YUGOSLAVIA	**28**	THAILAND
13	HUNGARY	**29**	KAMPUCHEA
14	ROMANIA	**30**	BRUNEI
15	BULGARIA	**31**	GAMBIA
16	ALBANIA	**32**	GUINEA-BISSAU

33	SIERRA LEONE
34	BURKINA FASO
35	TOGO
36	BENIN
37	EQUATORIAL
	GUINEA
38	CENTRAL AFRICAN
	REPUBLIC
39	UGANDA
40	RWANDA
41	BURUNDI
42	MALAWI
43	ZIMBABWE
44	BOTSWANA
45	SWAZILAND
46	LESOTHO

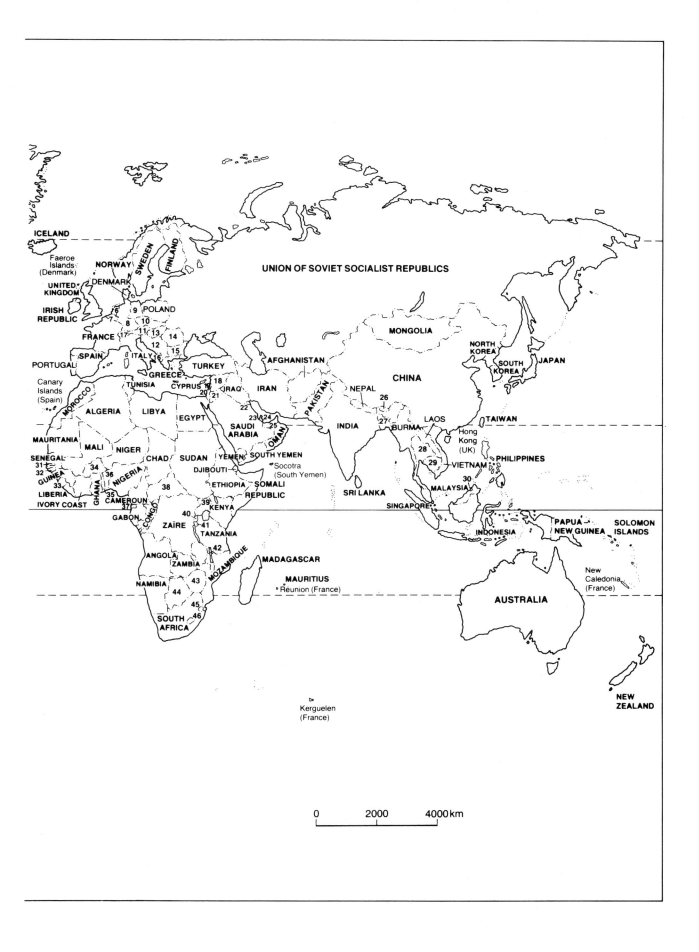

ICELAND

Faeroe
Islands
(Denmark)

NORWAY

SWEDEN

FINLAND

UNION OF SOVIET SOCIALIST REPUBLICS

UNITED
KINGDOM

DENMARK

IRISH
REPUBLIC

6

9 POLAND

7

8 10

11 13 14

FRANCE 17

12 15

SPAIN

ITALY 16

MONGOLIA

NORTH
KOREA

JAPAN

SOUTH
KOREA

PORTUGAL

GREECE

TURKEY

AFGHANISTAN

CHINA

Canary
Islands
(Spain)

TUNISIA

CYPRUS 18

MOROCCO

CYPRUS IRAQ

IRAN

NEPAL

26

TAIWAN

20 21

22

ALGERIA

LIBYA

EGYPT

23 24

25

PAKISTAN

INDIA

27 BURMA

LAOS

Hong
Kong
(UK)

MAURITANIA

SAUDI
ARABIA

OMAN

28

PHILIPPINES

MALI

NIGER

29

VIETNAM

SENEGAL

31

CHAD

SUDAN

YEMEN

SOUTH YEMEN

30

32

34

Socotra
(South Yemen)

MALAYSIA

GUINEA

33

36

DJIBOUTI

SRI LANKA

SINGAPORE

LIBERIA

35

NIGERIA

38

ETHIOPIA

SOMALI
REPUBLIC

IVORY COAST

CAMEROUN

37

PAPUA
NEW GUINEA

SOLOMON
ISLANDS

GABON

40

KENYA

39

CONGO

ZAÏRE

41

TANZANIA

INDONESIA

ANGOLA

42

New
Caledonia
(France)

ZAMBIA

MOZAMBIQUE

MADAGASCAR

NAMIBIA

43

MAURITIUS

Réunion (France)

AUSTRALIA

44

45

SOUTH
AFRICA

46

Kerguelen
(France)

NEW
ZEALAND

0   2000   4000km

I

1 Our violent world

In May 1968 serious rioting broke out in Paris: students face to face with police

1.1 Our violent age

Are we so violent today?

Open a newspaper, listen to the news on the radio, or watch a television news bulletin almost any day and you will be sure to be told about violence somewhere. Is the world becoming more violent? Or are we just becoming more aware of wars, revolutions and terrorism because the news media emphasize them so much?

It is true that the history of the human race is full of incidents of fighting and bloodshed. But even though there have been two World Wars in this century, we have been spared any conflict on such a widespread scale since 1945.

Indications of violence

On the other hand, there are three reasons for describing our own age as an age of violence:

  1 Man now has the power to destroy all life because of nuclear weapons (see chapter 2). The whole world lives in fear of this danger.

  2 The number of separate countries in the world has increased during the past 25 years as colonies have become independent. As a result wars and violence are more likely to break out:

a) Each new government has created its own armed forces and equipped them with modern weapons (see p. 9).

Our violent age

b) Several new countries have fought wars with their neighbours about their frontiers (such as India v. Pakistan, Israel v. Arab countries).
c) New governments have not always been accepted by their people. Some governments have killed large numbers in an effort to improve their authority (such as China, Indonesia, Kampuchea, Uganda). In other countries there have been civil wars (for example Nigeria, Pakistan, Algeria).

3 Countries of the world are geared up for fighting:
a) There are more than 18 million full-time soldiers in the world's armies.
b) There are 60 000 combat aircraft in the world's air forces.
c) The countries of the world spent $700 000 000 000 on their armies, navies and air forces in 1982.

Causes of violence

Why is the world such a violent place? This is a very difficult question to answer. Here are a few ideas to think about:

1 Men have always fought and killed each other. Is it in man's nature to be violent?

2 A few individuals enjoy power and will kill to gain and keep control of the government of a country.

3 People fight especially for their race, nation and religion. They will fight to defend and to expand them.

4 The riches of the world are very unevenly distributed. People will fight to gain more.

5 The more weapons there are the greater the likelihood that they will be used; and the more destructive they are, the more people who will be killed.

1.2 Violent change of government

In countries like Britain people can vote regularly in elections to change the government. But in many countries of the world this is not so. If people become particularly angry with their governments in these countries, they can only change them by force. There are basically four ways to do this:

1 revolt;
2 revolution;
3 civil war;
4 coup d'état.

One of the most famous revolutionary leaders in the Third World is Fidel Castro. He overthrew the hated dictator of Cuba, Batista, in 1959. The picture shows the bearded Castro waving to the enthusiastic crowd as he drives through the capital, Havana

Violent change of government

Revolts

People demonstrate and riot to demand a change of government or, at least, a very thorough change in the way the government is running the country.

In Western Europe in recent years there has been only one serious revolt of this kind. This took place in Paris in 1968. Students and workers made barricades in the streets and pelted the police with cobble-stones. It was several days before law and order were restored. The people were protesting against the government of President de Gaulle. He resigned the following year.

In Eastern Europe there have been many more revolts because it is so much more difficult to bring about changes in these countries. Since the 1950s there have been serious revolts in East Germany, Hungary, Czechoslovakia and, several times, in Poland (see p. 54).

Revolutions

Revolts are uprisings which, if they succeed, can bring about just a few changes. Revolutions are uprisings which bring about a complete change of government. Some people call the events in Hungary in 1956 a revolution because there was a complete change of government, if only for a short time.

Most of the revolutions in recent years have been uprisings of people in countries in Asia and Africa against the control of colonial countries. Some examples are the revolutions in Indo-China against the French; in Angola and Mozambique against the Portuguese; in Aden (now South Yemen) against the British.

One of the most famous revolutions was in Cuba where the people rose up against their own hated government. The story is really quite dramatic.

In 1958 a small number of exiles from Cuba landed back in their own country by boat. Their leader was Fidel Castro. It was a daring plan, but it paid off. The poor people of Cuba, mainly peasants, flocked to support him. They were then able to defeat the government soldiers and, in January 1959, they took over control.

Civil wars

Sometimes when an uprising takes place not all the people support the revolution. The fighting between the two sides can last for quite a long time, especially when many of the soldiers remain loyal to the government. There might even be battles between the forces of the government and the forces opposed to the government. This is called a 'civil war'. Civil wars can be particularly tragic since people who know each other, even relations, may be fighting on opposite sides.

Most recent civil wars have happened in Africa. The most serious was in Nigeria in the late 1960s. This took place because of tribal rivalries – a particular problem in Africa. The Ibo people in the south-eastern part tried to create their own, separate country of Biafra. The government army defeated them in a most bloody civil war.

Coups d'état

'Coup d'état' (pronounced 'coo-day-ta') is a French phrase for which there is no exact English translation. It is sometimes abbreviated to 'coup'. It is used to describe the taking over of a government by force.

Usually a group of soldiers occupy government buildings and arrest leaders of the government. Then the leaders of the coup announce that they are the new government. To prevent civil war between the two groups, deposed leaders are often put in prison or killed by the new government.

Many African countries have found it difficult in recent years to develop good governments. So quite often army leaders have taken over control by coups. The trouble is, once the army has taken over, it is difficult to arrange a return to government by civilians and parliament.

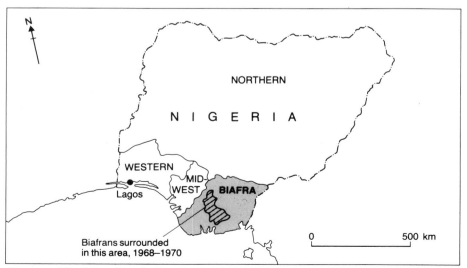

Map 1   The Nigerian civil war

1.3 Terrorism

Terrorists around the world

There is, sadly, nothing very new about fighting, riots, and revolutions. However, a form of violence which is fairly new in the world and which has become very common in recent years, is terrorism. This is the use of violence or the threat of violence by small groups of people to try to force governments to give in to their demands.

Terrorist groups

There are now about 150 terrorist groups in the world. They can be roughly divided into two kinds:

1 People who believe that their own government allows too little freedom to its citizens. Recent examples of these have been:
a) the Tupamaros in Uruguay;
b) the Angry Brigade in Britain;
c) the West German Red Army faction;
d) the Red Army in Japan;
e) the Red Brigades in Italy.

2 People who want their land freed from what they believe is foreign occupation. Recent examples of these have been:
a) the Front de Libération du Québec (FLQ) – French Canadians, who want Quebec to be separated from the rest of Canada;
b) the Irish Republican Army (IRA) – Irish Catholics who want Northern Ireland to be united with the Irish Republic;
c) ETA – the Basque people of northern Spain who want to be separated from the rest of Spain;
d) the Armenian Secret Army for the Liberation of Armenia (ASALA) – Armenia is a land which straddles the frontiers of modern Turkey, Russia and Iran. The people have been persecuted in the past, especially by the Turks;
e) the Popular Front for the Liberation of Palestine (PFLP) – Palestinians who have had their country taken away from them by Israel and who want a country of their own again. This was the main group in the Entebbe incident (see over).

In 1981 some IRA prisoners went on hunger strike. Several died, including Bobby Sands, whose funeral is shown here. The guard of honour are firing a salute

Terrorism

The Entebbe incident

Here is a famous example. In June 1976 a French airliner was making a flight from Tel Aviv in Israel to Paris. It made a stop at Athens. When it took off again it was carrying over 200 passengers. A few of these were terrorists.

As soon as they were in the air the terrorists 'hijacked' the aeroplane. That is, by threatening the crew and passengers with guns, they forced the pilot to change course. They directed him to fly to Entebbe airport in Uganda. When they arrived, the terrorists held the crew and passengers hostage in the airport buildings. They said they would kill them if other terrorists in prisons in various countries were not released. Most of the passengers were Israelis.

The Israeli army then undertook

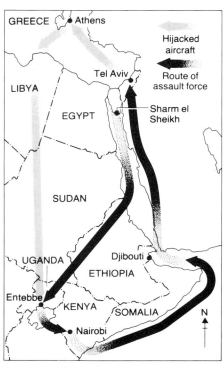

Map 2   The Entebbe incident, 1976

an incredible rescue operation. Specially trained soldiers were flown to Entebbe. They took the terrorists and Ugandan soldiers guarding the airport completely by surprise. They released the hostages, escorted them to their transport aircraft, and flew them back to safety in Israel.

Methods terrorists use

The hijacking of aeroplanes is only one of the methods that terrorists use. The following table shows the others.

	individuals	groups
capture	kidnapping	hijacking
murder	assassination	mass killing

In 1970 three airliners were hijacked by Palestinians in Jordan: passengers being addressed before the aircraft were blown up

Terrorism

Let us look briefly at each of these methods used by terrorists.

Capture

1 *Kidnapping.* Terrorists sometimes kidnap an important person such as a politician and hide him/her in a secret place. They threaten to kill their victims if the government does not agree to whatever they demand. Some of the most notorious kidnapping incidents have involved the FLQ , the Tupamaros and the Red Brigades.

2 *Hijacking.* In the 1960s and 1970s terrorists were frequently hijacking airliners. Having smuggled bombs or guns on board the terrorists would threaten to kill the passengers if their demands were not met. Often the hijackers wanted to escape to a friendly country, so the pilot would be forced to fly there instead of his proper destination, as in the Entebbe incident (p. 6).

The PFLP were involved in some of the most famous hijackings. Also Libya has been very willing to receive terrorists 'on the run', because the President, Colonel Qaddafy, believes that most terrorists are justified in their actions.

Murder

1 *Assassination.* Occasionally terrorists kill a particular person. They usually pick someone important, mainly to get maximum publicity. The most famous person to be killed in this way in recent years was Lord Mountbatten, a British admiral and uncle of the Queen. He was killed by an IRA bomb while on holiday in Ireland. The West German Red Army Faction is another group responsible for some particularly notorious assassinations.

2 *Mass killing.* Sometimes terrorists leave bombs fixed to explode at a particular time in a crowded place, such as a railway station. People who happen to be there at the time are killed or injured. This is, of course, a particularly vicious act. ETA, the IRA and the Red Brigades in particular have killed many people by bombs. One of the worst terrorist acts in Europe was a bomb at Bologna station in Italy in 1980. It killed 76 people and injured 185 (see extract p. 12).

A security guard, disguised as an athlete, after terrorists had killed Israeli competitors at the Munich Olympics, 1972

Reasons for terrorism

Why do terrorists use such cruel methods to try to get what they want? And what is it they want in any case?

Why use violence?

There are some extreme groups who believe the only way to fight evil in the world is by using violence, like the Shi'ite Muslim Al-Da'wa Movement and the Japanese Red Army, for example.

However, most groups have more specific aims. They are themselves suffering from injustice and cruelty, or at least they think so. They call themselves 'freedom fighters'. They believe that terrorist methods are the only ways they can use to fight back and improve the conditions they are complaining about. The question is, can terrorist methods *ever* be justified?

What do terrorists want?

Since a government never knows when and where they will strike next, the terrorists hope they will keep the government on constant tenterhooks. And so they hope in this way to wear down the government's will to resist their demands.

Particular acts of terrorism are sometimes planned to extract particular concessions. Sometimes the terrorists want the release of some of their comrades who have been caught and imprisoned. Sometimes they want publicity on television or in the newspapers for their cause. Why is publicity so important for terrorists? As long as their actions are reported, the public in general cannot forget their grievances.

1.4 Police and security

Violence by security forces

It is the reponsibility of the government of a country to keep law and order. The police and the army are used for this purpose.

However, it is sometimes thought that even the security forces themselves use too much violence in dealing with their opponents.

The amount of violence used by the police and the army differs very much from country to country. In countries like the USA, Australia, Britain, and in Western Europe the police are much less brutal than in Central and South America, Eastern Europe, and South Africa, for example.

Organization of security

In many countries there are three types of security forces to deal with different levels of disorder:
1 the police;
2 the riot police;
3 the army.

The need for information

In order to be ready for trouble and also to catch people who have been involved in violent actions, the security forces need information. They need:
1 information about people;
2 information about plans for violent action;
3 proof for convictions.
Security forces obtain this kind of information in various ways, but the most controversial and common method is the use of torture.

West German police disperse demonstrators with water-cannon in Bremen, 1980

Torture

The use of torture by governments against their opponents is very widespread. In recent years many thousands of people have suffered the most horrible agonies and mutilations, often leading to death. The countries most notorious for using torture are in Latin America and some in Africa.

But even Britain, which has a good tradition of humane treatment of prisoners, has used some mild forms of torture in Northern Ireland against the IRA. Here is a description by one victim:

‘ We were led into a building and eventually into a room where I was made to stand in a search position against a wall. My position was the same as for other men – fully stretched, hands as far apart as humanly possible and feet as far from the wall as possible. Back rigid and head held up. Not allowed to relax any of the joints at all. . . . I could not say how many times I collapsed. Initially my hands and legs were beaten whenever this happened and the insides of my feet were kicked until my ankles were swollen to almost twice their size. . . . I cannot possibly estimate for what duration I was against this wall and underwent the collapsing experiences and physical torture against this wall, but I would estimate that it must have been at least two full days and nights. During all of the time no sleep was permitted. . . . I was certainly verging on complete mental exhaustion, suffering delusions which were of nightmarish quality. ’

Imprisonment without trial

In some countries it is quite common for security forces to imprison suspects without putting them on trial in courts of law. In Russia, the secret police have put some people into mental hospitals. They are then given drugs which make them mentally deranged even though they were not when they entered the hospital.

Police and security

Protection

In recent years security forces have increased security precautions a great deal for protection against terrorists. For example, government buildings and crowded public places like museums and airports have security forces and metal-detection devices. It would now be very difficult, perhaps even impossible, to smuggle a bomb or a gun into the House of Commons or on to an aeroplane at Heathrow, for example. And, of course, important people have bodyguards.

Security methods

Equipment

Street riots have become so common that most security forces now have special equipment to disperse crowds. These include tear-gas (see also photograph, p. 143), plastic bullets and water-cannon. They are used when a crowd cannot be dispersed by baton-charges.

Training

Surprise and speed are essential in many security operations. One of the trickiest problems that security forces have to deal with is the release of hostages. We have seen how a brilliant operation rescued the hostages at Entebbe (p. 6). The highly trained British army units, the SAS (Special Air Service), are some of the most skilled. The timing and methods used to attack a building where hostages are held must be worked out extremely carefully; otherwise the terrorists would kill the hostages.

SAS squad storm the Iranian Embassy in London in 1980 to release hostages

1.5 Arms sales

Increase in arms sales

Terrorists use quite a wide variety of weapons: hand-guns, machine-guns, grenades, bombs, even small rocket-launchers. How do they obtain these? Unhappily in the world today if you have the money you can buy almost any weapon you wish. There are people, companies and countries that are making large profits by the sale of arms.

Only a small proportion goes to terrorists. The very big purchases in recent years have been made by the Third World countries of Asia, the Middle East and Africa. These countries particularly want to build up their armies. The biggest suppliers are America, Russia and France. The cartoon shows how the sale of really big weapons like missiles, tanks, aircraft and warships has increased in recent years.

Effects of arms sales

Such arms sales have several unfortunate effects:

1 Quite poor countries spend a lot of money on arms, which might otherwise be used to improve their standards of living.

2 When weapons are sold it is impossible to tell how they might be used. For example, when Britain and Argentina were at war over the Falkland Islands in 1982, one of the warships used by Argentina had been bought from Britain some years before. And British ships were sunk by Exocet missiles which the Argentinians had bought from France, one of Britain's allies.

3 The great number of wars fought in recent years have been made possible by the international sale of arms. Countries cannot fight wars if they have no weapons.

Increase in arms sales, 1968–82

1.6 Recent wars

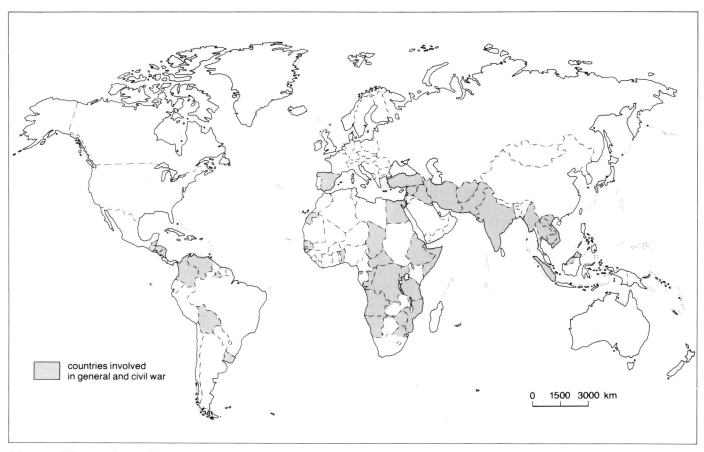

Map 3   Wars in the world, 1973–83

A world of wars

During this century there have been two World Wars when the most powerful countries fought each other. Since 1945 when the Second World War ended there has not been another war like it. The most powerful countries are now the United States and Russia. They have been frightened to fight each other in case war between them turns into a nuclear war (see chapters 2 and 3).

But does this mean that the world has been at peace since 1945? Far from it.

Different kinds of wars

There have, in fact, been about 200 wars since 1945. The only parts of the world which have not been involved in war have been the Arctic, Antarctic and Australasia.

Why have wars been fought?

Some of the wars since 1945 have, in fact, been fought by the big countries, but against other smaller countries, not each other. Many of the wars in recent years have been fought to:

1 remove colonial rulers;
2 overthrow hated governments;
3 gain control of particular areas of land.

There have been so many changes in governments and the control of various parts of the world that so many wars have been almost inevitable. In particular, there are now far more separate countries in the world than there were in 1945.

There are therefore more countries to quarrel with each other.

Some examples

Here are some examples of the main kinds of wars in recent years:

1 Wars fought by the USA and Russia: the Americans fought in Korea in the 1950s and Vietnam in the 1960s; Russia has been fighting in Afghanistan since the late 1970s.

2 Wars to remove the colonial rulers: for example against the French in Algeria in 1954–62.

3 Civil wars between different peoples making up a newly independent country, such as the Biafran war in Nigeria in the late 1960s (see p. 4).

4 Wars between countries about the ownership of particular areas of land: such as the wars between India

Recent wars

and Pakistan in 1947/8, 1965, 1971; between Britain and Argentina over the Falkland Islands in 1982.

5 Wars fought over the very existence of Israel as a new, non-Arab country in an Arab area of the world.

6 Fighting to overthrow a hated government: for example, the Hungarian uprising of 1956.

The cost and suffering of wars

Wars cost huge sums of money. For example, the war in Vietnam, which admittedly lasted a long time (13 years), cost the Americans $170 000 000 000! Just imagine how that money might have been used to improve people's standards of health and living conditions.

Wars also, of course, involve immense human suffering. In civil wars and wars which are waged over large areas, civilians as well as soldiers, sailors and airmen are killed and wounded. Wars also uproot people from their homes making them refugees.

Scores of millions of people have

It is estimated that the Falklands war cost Britain about £2 billion. 'HMS Sheffield' pictured ablaze here was one of the ships destroyed

been seriously affected by war since 1945 – they have either been killed, or wounded, had relations killed, had their homes destroyed, or been made refugees. Probably about 10 million people have been killed and about 40

million made refugees since 1945. So violence, originally undertaken to improve human conditions, has made life much worse for most of mankind.

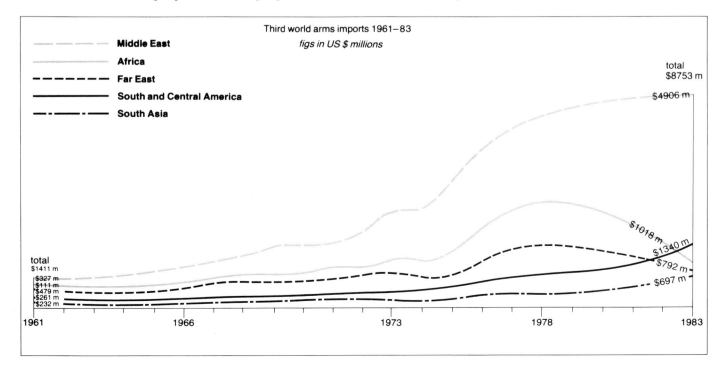

Third world arms imports 1961–83

figs in US $ millions

Middle East

Africa

Far East

South and Central America

South Asia

total $8753 m

$4906 m

$1018 m

$1340 m

$792 m

$697 m

total $1411 m

$327 m
$111 m
$479 m
$261 m
$232 m

1961   1966   1973   1978   1983

Questions

1 **a** How much money was spent on the armed forces of the world *per day* in 1982?

   b Why was there a civil war in Nigeria in the late 1960s?

   c What is the difference between a 'revolt' and a 'revolution'?

   d Name four terrorist groups from different continents of the world.

   e What are the four main methods used by terrorists?

   f Why do you think terrorists use the methods they do?

   g Why do security forces use torture?

   h Over what islands did Britain fight Argentina in 1982?

   i Why do you think there have been so many wars since 1945?

2 Write an essay or hold a class discussion on when, if ever, fighting and killing are justified.

3 Study the graph on page 11 and answer the questions.

   a Which region of the Third World spent most on arms: (i) in 1961?; (ii) in 1983?

   b What proportion of the total Third World expenditure on arms in 1983 was spent by the countries of the Middle East?

   c In what year did spending on arms by Third World countries increase particularly steeply? Can you explain why?

4 Read the following newspaper report and answer the questions.

‘   The spectre of international terrorism is haunting Europe more than ever, despite some recent bloody victories over hijackers and hostage-takers.

One chilling statistic was produced at this week's Council of Europe terrorism conference where experts, politicians, and policemen debated and sometimes bickered over what to do about it. There are more than 150 terrorist groups in the world, and, according to a recent CIA report, West Europe is their major stamping ground. Of all the world terrorist incidents in the last decade (*10 years*), 38 per cent took place there. All experts agree the number is increasing.

This year alone has seen Libyan and Iraqi-backed murder squads settling scores in London and Paris; the occupation of Iranian embassies; and a small but alarming stream of the usual killings in Northern Ireland.

In Spain, the Basque separatists of ETA were reportedly being trained this year by Palestinians in Yemen. In Italy, after 76 corpses from the August Bologna railway station explosion, and in Paris after the recent synagogue blast, the victims of the Right are piling up. On the other hand, it was the left-wing Red Brigade who killed a Milan businessman only last Wednesday.

. . . the reaction of Euro-governments is taking on a definite pattern – fierce domestic anti-terrorist laws; a quiet increase in police and military and intelligence links; hesitant moves towards the end of international sanctuary for "political" crimes, and a tendency to call for censorship.   ’

The Guardian, 15 November, 1980

   a Which part of the world has suffered most from terrorism in the 1970s?

   b What do you think 'separatists' are? (see p. 5).

   c Which government measures to combat terrorism (listed in the final paragraph) are likely to be most effective? Why?

5 Read the following passage and answer the questions.

‘   GENOCIDE is an ugly word. It is the name given to the biggest crime man is capable of. After years of study, some of the world's best legal brains assisted in drawing up the definition written into the United Nations Convention on Genocide:

"In the present Convention genocide means any of the following acts committed with intent to destroy, in whole or in part, a national, ethnical, racial or religious group, as such:
   a. Killing of members of the group;
   b. Causing serious bodily or mental harm to members of the group;
   c. Deliberately inflicting on the group conditions of life calculated to bring about its physical destruction in whole or in part;
   d. Imposing measures intended to prevent births within the group;
   e. Forcibly transferring children of the group to another group.
Obviously, in time of war men get killed. It is the use of the phrase 'with intent' that separates the usual casualties inflicted during war from the crime of genocide."   ’

Frederick Forsyth, *The Making of an African Legend: The Biafra Story* (1977)

a What is 'Genocide'?

b What is the meaning of the phrase 'with intent'? Why do you think it is important?

2 The threat of nuclear doom

July 1946, at Bikini Atoll, the Pacific: tests of atomic weapons – shown here is an explosion beneath a fleet of ships

2.1 What nuclear weapons do

The power of a nuclear bomb

Just picture, if you can, the mutilation, death and devastation that would be caused by the dropping of a nuclear bomb or missile over central London. The area likely to be affected is shown on map 1.

Within three seconds a fire-ball would be formed with the intensity of heat of the inside of the sun. People in the open beneath the fire-ball would be vaporized – that is, simply disappear. Even seven miles away fires would rage and people's flesh would be charred with third-degree burns.

Within twelve seconds the blast waves, creating winds twice the speed of a hurricane, would smash buildings over a five-mile radius, fires would be fanned by the wind, cars tossed about.

Within ten minutes a great mushroom cloud about six miles in radius, would be formed, which would then shower radio-active dust. Some of this would be scattered over a wide area, depending on the wind.

How have these weapons, whose energy comes from the tiniest particles of matter, come to be such an horrific threat?

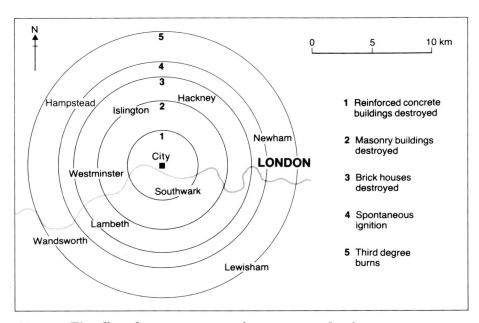

Map 1   The effect of a one-megaton nuclear weapon on London

What nuclear weapons do

How 'the bomb' works

Nuclear weapons are often talked about as 'the bomb', even though most are carried as warheads on missiles.

The two kinds of bomb

As we shall see later, nuclear weapons are built in many different sizes. But whatever the size, a nuclear weapon works on one of two basic systems. First of all we need to understand these.

Atomic bombs and 'fission'

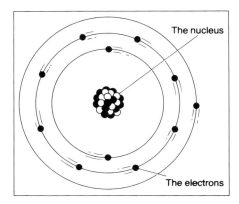

Fig 1   Structure of the atom

All matter is made up of minute particles called 'atoms'. As you can see from figure 1, an atom is itself made up of a nucleus and surrounding electrons. The nucleus is made up of protons and neutrons. The weapons we are discussing here are called 'atomic', or 'nuclear', weapons because their power comes from the energy released when the pattern of an *atom*, or *nucleus*, is changed in particular ways.

The atoms of some very *heavy* elements can be made to split. This is called 'fission' (see figure 2). When this happens intense heat and radioactivity are produced. The two heavy elements used in this way in bombs are uranium and plutonium. These bombs are sometimes called 'atomic' or 'A-bombs'.

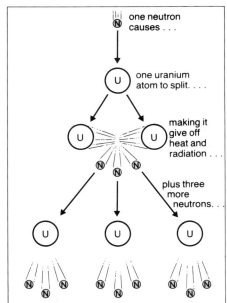

Fig 2   Nuclear reaction: Fission

Hydrogen bombs and 'fusion'

Just as some heavy elements split, so also some *light* elements can be made to join together. This is called 'fusion' (see figure 3). When this happens even greater heat is produced. In fact, this is the way the sun produces its heat. So this is called a thermo-nuclear bomb

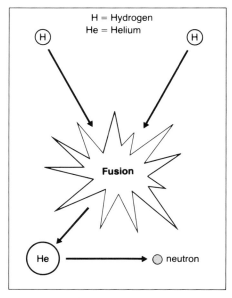

Fig 3   Nuclear reaction: Fusion

('thermo' meaning heat). The two light elements used in this way in bombs are hydrogen and lithium. These bombs are also called hydrogen or H-bombs.

But the only way the fusion can be made to happen is by intense heat. In a thermo-nuclear weapon this 'trigger' heat is provided by a uranium or plutonium fission explosion. The diagrams may help you to understand these reactions more clearly.

Effects of a nuclear explosion

Immediate effects

A nuclear weapon is not just a big bomb. Unlike a high-explosive bomb, it produces three separate effects.

1 *Blast.*   This is the same effect as a high-explosive bomb only much more powerful. The large nuclear weapons produce a blast wave of such power that, as we have seen, it is capable of killing people and demolishing buildings over a radius of many miles.

2 *Heat.*   The heat produced by a nuclear explosion is intense (see p. 13): people close to the point of explosion would be vaporized, others would suffer fearful burns. The heat would also cause many fires to break out.

3 *Radiation.*   When a nuclear weapon explodes a great amount of debris is sucked high into the air to form a massive mushroom-shaped cloud (see the photograph on p. 13). This debris is poisoned by the radiation released in the explosion and falls as radioactive dust. This fall-out may last for many days and cover a very wide area. Radiation is rather like X-rays and can be very dangerous to all forms of life. Large

What nuclear weapons do

doses kill instantly. People with smaller doses suffer radiation sickness before dying. If the dosage is very mild, they eventually recover. People with radiation sickness suffer from vomiting, diarrhoea, loss of hair and internal bleeding.

Long-term effects

Radioactivity also has frightening long-term effects. There is no way of making radioactive material harmless. It is a matter of waiting until the radioactivity gradually decays. In the case of some elements this may take very many years. It is also possible for the reproductive

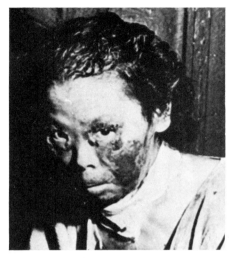

A burned survivor of the Hiroshima bomb

organs to be affected even in people who might otherwise appear perfectly healthy. As a result people may become sterile or give birth to deformed babies. What is more, deformities can be passed on to later generations.

Also, because of the dust which would be thrown into the atmosphere, the sun would be partially blotted out. This would affect the climate and therefore agriculture. The world would be plunged into a 'nuclear winter'

2.2 Nuclear weapons and how they can be delivered

The variety of nuclear weapons

Size

The power of a nuclear weapon is measured in the equivalent weight in tons of ordinary explosive, TNT. 'Kilo' means thousand and 'mega' means million.

At the start of this chapter we described the likely effects of a weapon dropped on London. These calculations have been made for a one-megaton bomb – that is the explosive power of 1 000 000 tons of TNT. Nuclear weapons have now been made in a wide variety of sizes, from a few kilotons to several megatons. They can be made as artillery shells, missile warheads or bombs.

Range

The countries which have produced these weapons have thought up different ways of using them:

1 *tactical* weapons – missiles or bombs for use on the battlefield,

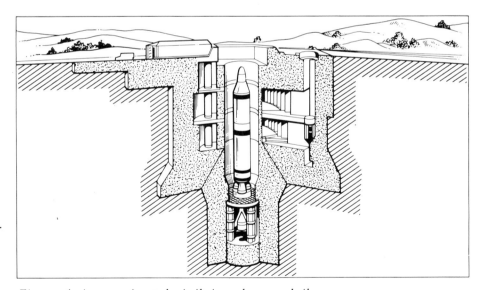

Fig 4   An intercontinental missile in underground silo

rather like artillery, though, of course, each missile would be thousands of times more destructive than an ordinary shell;

2 *theatre* weapons – for use by one country against another;

3 *strategic* weapons – for use over great distances, between continents.

Ways of delivery

Missiles

The most common form of delivering a nuclear weapon to its target is a rocket-propelled missile. Missiles travel so fast that it is almost impossible to shoot them down. Again, missiles vary in size

Nuclear weapons and how they can be delivered

depending on the range for which they are designed. They can be launched from trucks, aeroplanes, ships or submarines. The largest, called ICBMs (inter-continental ballistic missiles), are launched from individual, protected underground silos, as you can see from figure 4 on page 15.

A very important consideration is to try to ensure that your own nuclear weapons are not destroyed by your enemy before you can hit his targets. How do you think this might be arranged? Three main ways have been invented:

1 *Submarine-launched ballistic missiles (SLBMs).* The easiest way to hide is in the depths of the ocean. So nuclear submarines have been built. These are powered by nuclear engines so that they can remain submerged for long periods of time.

2 *Multiple independently targeted re-entry vehicles (MIRVs).* A missile can now be fitted with several warheads. It can release these so that they can follow their own separate routes to their own separate targets. MIRVs have another advantage:

The launching of a 'Trident' missile from a submerged submarine

even if only one missile survives an attack by an enemy, that one can launch, say, eight nuclear weapons on to enemy targets.

3 *Cruise missiles.* These are pilotless jet-propelled flying bombs.

They can fly so low and by such indirect routes that it is difficult either to detect them or to know what their likely targets might be.

A cruise missile convoy leaves its base at Greenham Common in Berkshire

Nuclear weapons and how they can be delivered

Aircraft

Unlike these weapons aeroplanes are quite easy to shoot down. However, they are still used for carrying nuclear weapons. Small, fast aircraft can be used to drop small bombs in a battlefield attack. Long-range attacks can be made by strategic bombers operating at a distance from an enemy country, for example, by releasing cruise missiles.

Fast, low-flying bombers like these FB-111s are designed to penetrate Soviet defences and drop nuclear weapons on to selected targets

2.3 Development of nuclear weapons

Dr J Robert Oppenheimer

The use of nuclear weapons and threats to use them

The first bomb

It was on 6 December 1941 that the American government decided that an atomic bomb should be made. The Second World War had already started and Hitler had conquered much of Europe. Scientists warned President Roosevelt that Hitler would be much more dangerous if Germany managed to build such a bomb first. So a team of brilliant scientists was gathered together under Robert Oppenheimer. On 16 July 1945 the first atomic bomb was exploded as a test in the wastes of the New Mexico desert. The scientists had not known exactly what to expect. Many were horrified at the terrible power they had unleashed. And, in fact, by now the war in Europe was over and Hitler was dead.

Hiroshima and Nagasaki

However, the war with Japan was still being fought. President Roosevelt was dead and the new President, Harry S Truman, had to decide whether to use atomic bombs on Japan. He ordered two bombs to be dropped – one on Hiroshima on 6 August 1945 and the other on Nagasaki three days later. By present-day standards these bombs were quite small – in the 20 kiloton range. Yet the effects were horrific. In Hiroshima three square miles and 60 000 houses were destroyed. About 75 000 people were killed instantly and over 100 000 more have died eventually from wounds, burns and radiation sickness.

Several eye-witnesses have described the horror of these explosions. One brief diary entry for Hiroshima on 9 August gives some impression of a few of the effects:

' Darkness came and still there were no lights except the lights from the fires where the dead were burned. And again, the smell of burning flesh. The hospital was quieter, but in the isolation ward, the stillness of the night was broken again and again by the little girl. '

Development of nuclear weapons

The devastation caused by the atomic bomb on Hiroshima 1945. These remains of the Industrial Promotion Building were preserved as a memorial and a warning

The bombs dropped on Hiroshima and Nagasaki are the only nuclear weapons that have been exploded in war. As new weapons have been developed, they have been tested. There have also been threats, alerts and alarms but, fortunately, these have not led to nuclear attacks.

The Cuban Missile Crisis

The most serious alert occurred in 1962. This was the Cuban Missile Crisis and provided a dreadful lesson in how a nuclear war might actually break out.

By that time the USA and Russia had been quarrelling for many years. Each side had built many nuclear weapons, with aeroplanes and missiles to deliver them.

In the Autumn of 1962 the Russian leader, Nikita Khrushchev, sent some missiles to Cuba – an island off the coast of the USA with a

government friendly towards Russia. Khrushchev probably had several reasons for doing this:

1 He wanted to bully the new, young American President, John Kennedy.

2 He wanted to help the Cuban Communist government which was being threatened by the Americans.

3 The USA had more nuclear weapons than Russia (some sited in Turkey, very close to Russia) and these extra missiles (see map 2) might help to balance out this unevenness.

Kennedy felt that he could not allow the missiles to stay in Cuba; Khrushchev felt that he could not back down once he had made the challenge.

The world learned of the Crisis on 22 September when Kennedy announced his discovery that the missiles were being put into position. The US navy blockaded Cuba. The world waited with bated breath.

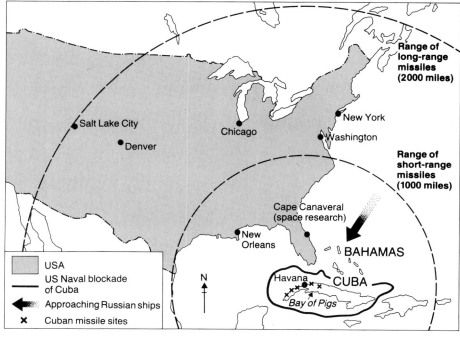

Map 2   The Cuban Missile Crisis, 1962

Development of nuclear weapons

Would the crisis lead to nuclear war? There were agonizing delays in the exchange of letters as there was no 'hot-line' teleprinter link between the two leaders at the time. Eventually a compromise agreement was reached. Khrushchev promised to remove the missiles; Kennedy agreed not to invade Cuba. The world could breathe more easily again.

Theories about nuclear war and peace

Superpower fears

Although (as we shall see on pp. 21–22) some other countries have nuclear weapons, America and Russia have by far the greatest stocks. These countries are so powerful that they are called 'superpowers'. Since the end of the Second World War in 1945 they have been suspicious and afraid of each other. Why do you think this has happened?

As we see in chapter 4, the Russian government believes in Communism. The Russians are afraid that the Americans want to destroy this system. These fears seem well-founded because it was the Americans who developed nuclear weapons and built up huge stocks first and also surrounded Russia with military bases, as you can see from map 3 on p. 56. On their side, the Americans have believed that the Russians are planning to spread Communism throughout the world. This fear also seems well-founded because the Communist theory says so and because Russian leaders have often repeated it

In order to extend their influence and to improve their defences, the two superpowers have each created

The Cuban Missile Crisis: an American warship and aircraft near Puerto Rico inspect a Soviet freighter carrying crated missiles

great military alliances (see map 3, p. 56). The Americans set up NATO (the *North Atlantic Treaty Organization*) in 1949 and the Russians replied with the *Warsaw Pact* in 1955. It is these two great military organizations that threaten each other with nuclear catastrophe.

Fortunately NATO and the Warsaw Pact have not come to blows. But each side has huge armies, navies and air forces and experts have devised elaborate plans to use them if war should break out. There are basically two plans – one to avoid nuclear war, the other to win a nuclear war. You can see these two plans illustrated by the cartoons on page 20.

Deterrence

The plan to avoid war is called 'deterrence' (see cartoon, over). The basic idea is that one side should have so many nuclear weapons that even if the enemy destroyed some, there would still be enough to cause so much destruction to the enemy that he would be too afraid to attack in the first place. He would be 'deterred'. From the mid-1950s to the mid-1970s both sides developed weapons in order to keep the balance of 'mutually assured destruction', or MAD for short! Russia and America could be sure of destroying each other. Bombers and missiles have been programmed to attack cities so as to make the other side frightened. Neither side could win a nuclear war so neither side would start one.

Development of nuclear weapons

Deterrence

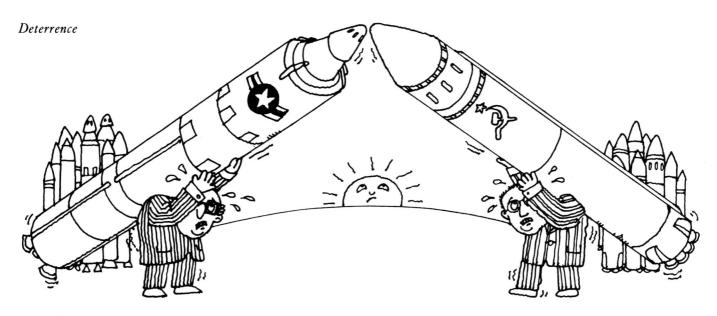

Nuclear war fighting

The alternative plan is to try to 'win' a nuclear war (see cartoon, below). This assumes that a nuclear war could be limited in its effects. It is then necessary to have a wide variety of weapons in order to fight different kinds of wars. The emphasis in this plan is on ways of using nuclear weapons first so as to gain the advantage. The main targets therefore are not cities, but the enemy's missile sites, military headquarters and so forth. The aim is to try to prevent the enemy from having any weapons left to hit back with.

From 1969 it seemed that NATO might well be the first to use nuclear weapons. NATO believed that because the Warsaw Pact had so many 'conventional' forces (that is non-nuclear weapons like tanks) the only way that a Warsaw Pact attack could be successfully resisted was with nuclear weapons. Then in 1980 President Carter of the USA issued orders that American nuclear forces should be aimed at Russian military targets rather than cities. It is possible that the Russians have made similar changes in their plans. However, the point is that by the early 1980s nuclear war seemed more likely than before. Some politicians and military leaders were perhaps planning not to *avoid* a nuclear war at all costs, but to *win* it should it break out – even though they were saying that deterrence was still their main plan.

'Winning' a nuclear war

Development of nuclear weapons

Stockpiles and the spread of nuclear weapons

Proliferation

It is estimated that there are now over 50 000 nuclear weapons in the world with a combined total power equivalent to about one million Hiroshima bombs. Only a fraction of these are needed to destroy all life on our planet. America and Russia have the vast majority of these. The cartoon (right) shows how many long-range weapons alone each of these countries had by 1981. The following countries also have nuclear weapons: Britain, France, China and India. It is suspected that Israel and South Africa have some. And several other countries may be developing

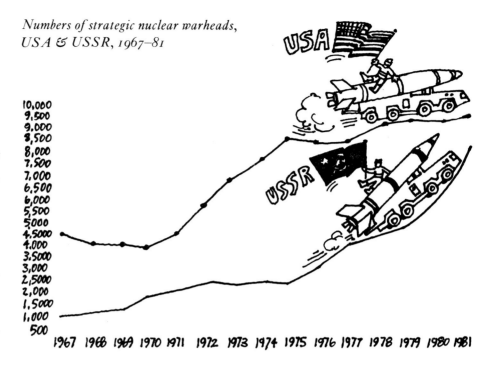

Numbers of strategic nuclear warheads, USA & USSR, 1967–81

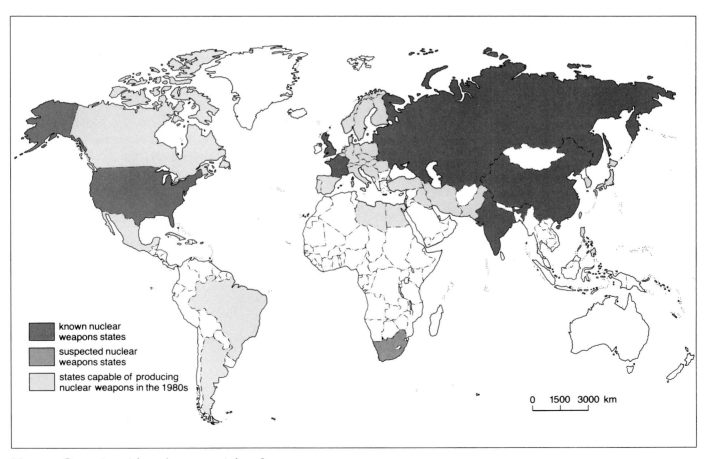

Map 3   Countries with nuclear potential, 1983

known nuclear weapons states

suspected nuclear weapons states

states capable of producing nuclear weapons in the 1980s

0   1500   3000 km

Development of nuclear weapons

American 'Minuteman' ICBMs being tested. The USA has about 1000 of these

Soviet ICBMs photographed at the Red Square parade in Moscow, 1974

their own: for example, Pakistan, Brazil, and Argentina. Of course, the more countries that have nuclear weapons, the greater the likelihood that a nuclear war will break out somewhere in the world. This spread of nuclear weapons is called 'proliferation'.

Delivery systems

The huge stockpiles of bombs and warheads built up by the Russians and Americans are fitted in the following delivery systems:

1 *Land-based missiles.* America's main strategic ICBM (inter-continental ballistic missile) is *Minuteman III.* These are MIRVed (see p. 16). Each carries the explosive power of 27 Hiroshima bombs and can be aimed so accurately that the warhead can land within an area smaller than a football pitch after a journey of 6000 miles. The Russians have three kinds of ICBMs, also MIRVed: SS-17, SS-18 and SS-19. Both countries also have modern medium-range or theatre missiles – the American *Pershing II* and the Russian SS-20.

2 *SLBMs* (see p.16). Both countries have hundreds of nuclear

Development of nuclear weapons

weapons in submarines constantly on patrol in the oceans. The Americans have *Poseidon* and *Trident*, the Russians have SS-N8 and SS-N18. *Trident*-armed submarines, for example, each have 192 nuclear warheads with a range of 4000 miles.

3 *Bombers.* The Americans have a lot of B-52 strategic bombers each able to carry four one-megaton bombs. The Russians have a few, older *Badger* and *Bison* bombers. Both countries have medium-range bombers: the Americans have the FB-111 and the Russians, the *Backfire*; both very modern designs.

4 *New weapons.* Research continues to develop weapons that are even more accurate and difficult to destroy. The Americans are developing a missile called MX ('missile, experimental') fitted with ten warheads, very accurate and designed to destroy Russian missile sites. There has been considerable argument in America about how MX missiles should be sited to ensure

American B-52s, used to bomb North Vietnam and now being modernized with cruise missiles

their own safety.

5 *'Star wars'.* In 1983 President Reagan ordered the start of a research programme to devise a system of using space vehicles or satellites for destroying intercontinental missiles in flight –

by using lasers or electro-magnetic power for example. Many scientists were sceptical about its practicability. Others were worried that such developments would frighten the Russians and make the world even more dangerous.

Taken at the Moscow air show: the large bomber in the foreground is a 'Bison'

2.4 Control and disarmament

Arrangements to control nuclear weapons

Reasons for worrying

As more and more nuclear weapons were made, so people became worried. Even testing bombs is dangerous because the radioactivity can pollute the atmosphere. For example, in 1954 some Japanese fishermen suffered radiation sickness because they were showered with radioactive dust from an American test explosion. They were fishing in the Pacific Ocean, supposedly a safe distance from the explosion. Also, as we saw on p. 21, an increasing number of countries have developed or plan to develop and test nuclear weapons. Then, in 1962 the Cuban Missile Crisis made many people very worried.

Why has agreement been difficult?

Politicians decided that, because people had become worried, they should try to reach agreement to control nuclear weapons. However, this has not been easy for a number of reasons.

Some countries without nuclear weapons think that those with them are wanting to keep this power to themselves. The Russians and the Americans are suspicious of each other. If one country disarms, it believes that the other will take advantage. If they both agree to disarm, the one fears that the other will cheat. It is true that by spying each country could check up on the other especially by using photography from satellites circling the earth. But the Americans and Russians could never be *absolutely* sure that the other side was not hiding some missiles somewhere.

The most important agreements

Despite these difficulties some agreements have been made. These are some of the most important.

1 *Partial Test-Ban Treaty, 1963.* All countries signing the treaty promised not to make any nuclear tests except underground, so as to avoid pollution. Over 100 countries signed, but not France or China, who have continued tests.

2 *Non-Proliferation Treaty, 1968.* Countries signing the treaty who had no nuclear weapons promised not to make or obtain them. Countries signing the treaty who had nuclear weapons promised not to help other countries to make or obtain them. Over 80 countries signed. But quite a large number who were obviously planning to obtain their own weapons have not, such as Israel, South Africa, Pakistan, and Brazil.

3 *Several 'Geographical Treaties'.* These treaties prohibit the testing or placing of nuclear weapons in the Antarctic, outer space, Latin American and on the sea-bed.

Control and disarmament

4 *Strategic Arms Limitation Talks (SALT).* Since the end of the 1960s the Americans and Russians have negotiated to keep down the various numbers of nuclear weapons. Sometimes the Americans and Russians seem more willing to co-operate with each other than at other times. When the tension between the two countries is relaxed this is called 'détente'. In 1972 Russia and America signed an Arms Limitation Treaty. It was intended to be the first of a series. It was therefore called SALT-I. The main agreement was to restrict the number of anti-missile missiles. SALT-II followed in 1979, but before it could be formally approved, Russia and America were quarrelling again.

Arms Reduction Talks

By the early 1980s talks were being held between the Americans and Russians on the reduction of long-range strategic weapons (START – *Strategic Arms Reduction Talks*) and medium-range weapons (INF – *Intermediate Nuclear Forces*). They ended (1983) without agreement; new talks began, 1985.

Nuclear disarmament

Unilateral or multilateral?

Most of the talks and treaties have been about preventing any more nuclear weapons being made rather than reducing the numbers. Yet many people wish to see nuclear weapons abolished altogether. This idea is called 'nuclear disarmament'.

It cannot, of course, be done by waving a magic wand. Either one government must decide to abolish its own nuclear weapons, or two or more must agree to do this together. The first is called 'unilateral disarmament'; the second, 'multilateral disarmament'.

Most people agree that multilateral disarmament is preferable. However, some people believe that nuclear weapons are so evil and dangerous that unilateral disarmament is better than no disarmament at all. For example, in Britain and America nuclear weapons exist as a protection against Russian Communism. However, unilateral disarmers believe that their own unilateral policy may lead eventually to multilateral disarmament; but that in any case it is 'better to be Red than dead'. ('Red' is often used in America to mean Communist.)

Throughout the 1960s there was an 'arms race' between the USA and the USSR and huge stocks of weapons were built up. In 1969 talks were started seeking agreement to slow down the competition. Eventually in 1972 Presidents Brezhnev and Nixon signed SALT-1. They are seen here celebrating the conclusion of the agreement in Moscow. However, many problems remained:

1 *Huge stocks of weapons still existed: there was no agreement to reduce numbers*
2 *Although SALT-1 was supposed to be the first of a series of treaties, the Russians and Americans quarrelled again especially from 1979 to 1984.*
3 *Further progress would be difficult if talks tried to distinguish between strategic (long-range) and intermediate range weapons: the negotiators could quarrel over these categories!*

Control and disarmament

CND and END

In 1957 an organization was set up in Britain called CND (the *Campaign for Nuclear Disarmament*). It took as its simple badge the semaphore code for the letters N and D. Politicians, writers, churchmen and many ordinary men and women joined the movement. They held meetings and organized rallies and marches. They hoped to persuade the Labour Party to accept unilateral disarmament. But this did not happen and the movement almost came to an end. Almost, but not quite.

In 1980 there was a revival – and a spread of the ideas to other West European countries in new movements including END (*European Nuclear Disarmament*). A similar movement also developed in the USA. People were becoming more frightened because, as we saw on p. 20, governments were now talking about *winning* rather than *avoiding* nuclear war. A number of demonstrations have taken place,

When CND was founded its main demonstrations were marches each Easter to and from the Atomic Weapons Research Establishment at Aldermaston in Berkshire

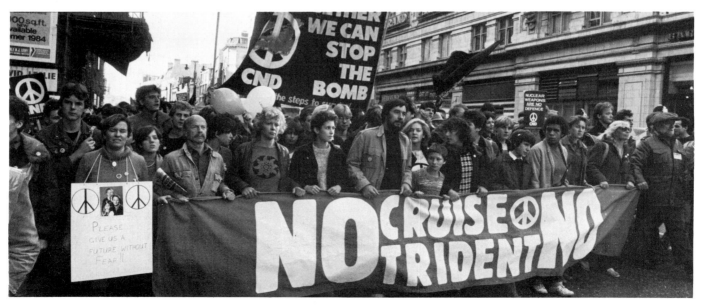

CND revived in the 1980s to protest against American cruise missiles in Britain and the British government's decision to buy Trident submarine missiles

Control and disarmament

especially in West Germany, against the placing of American weapons in these countries.

Britain's special position

There has been much opposition to nuclear weapons in Britain. Why do you think this is so? In the first place, Britain was the third country (after America and Russia) to develop nuclear weapons and so has had them for many years now. They are very expensive and other countries with the technology, such as West Germany and Italy, do not have them. In addition, the Americans have had their own aeroplanes and nuclear weapons in Britain for many years so that Britain has become, in some people's view, an American 'aircraft carrier'. In particular, plans to place cruise missiles (see p. 16) in Britain have led to very passionate demonstrations from 1982. Much of the protest was undertaken by women who camped at Greenham Common in Berkshire where the missiles are stationed.

But most seriously, many people believe that Britain could be very easily and quickly wiped out in a nuclear attack. It has been calculated that about 200 megatons would be needed to destroy all vital targets in Britain (see map 4). This is a tiny fraction of Russia's nuclear stockpile, but 1000 times the amount of explosive dropped by the Germans on Britain during the whole of the Second World War. If the country is in such danger and that danger can be avoided by giving up nuclear weapons, then why, you might well ask, doesn't the government do it? The answer is, of course, that there are arguments on the other side too.

Map 4   Soviet map showing what the major targets in Britain would be in the case of nuclear war

Greenham Common, Berkshire; women demonstrators face police. The women have camped outside the cruise missile base for many months in protest against cruise missiles being based in Britain

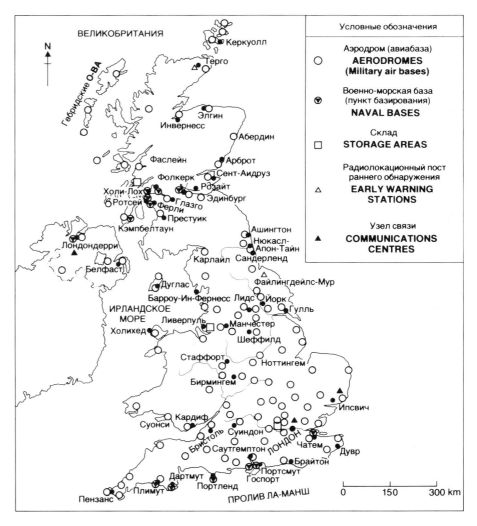

27

2.5 Arguments for and against nuclear weapons

Arguments for

Belief in deterrence

There are, in fact, very strong arguments in favour of nuclear weapons. Ever since the late 1940s the two superpowers, the USA and Russia, have been quarrelling. Yet they have not actually gone to war with each other. Many people believe that their quarrels would have led to war – to a Third World War – if they had not been so frightened of the effects of nuclear weapons. In other words, deterrence has worked. Furthermore, many people believe that it can only continue to work if the two sides are roughly in balance. If one side disarms this will disturb that balance, and the other side might well take advantage.

Fear of blackmail

After all, if a country has no nuclear weapons at all, any country which does have nuclear weapons could make demands on pain of nuclear attack – a sort of international mugging. You can see how this might happen from the cartoon.

Arguments against

Expense

On the other hand, there are strong arguments against nuclear weapons. By the early 1980s the world was spending over $500 000 000 000 per year on armed forces! It is true that only a portion of this vast sum was spent on nuclear weapons and that conventional weapons are also very expensive. Nevertheless, just think how much human starvation, malnutrition, illness and misery could have been relieved by using even a fraction of this money to help the poorer countries of the world. You might therefore say that the world is poorer because of nuclear weapons.

Unthinkable terror

Is the world also more dangerous because of nuclear weapons? Several people have had nightmare visions of a nuclear war starting by accident. In an age of missiles this is particularly serious because reactions and decisions must be made in matters of minutes, even seconds.

But the most serious argument of all against nuclear weapons is the utter horror of what a full-scale nuclear attack on, say Britain would mean. Try to imagine what it would mean in sheer human terms, let alone the colossal damage to buildings.

Millions of people would be killed instantly. The survivors would envy them. For many of the survivors would be suffering unbearable injuries, burns and radiation sickness. The medical services that survived the attack would be utterly overwhelmed by the huge numbers needing attention. Other services would also be affected, many would be destroyed or break down: electricity, gas, water, sewerage, food supplies.

The country would collapse into a fierce anarchy. Only the physically unscathed and toughest could endure this, and then only if they could cope with the mental strain that the struggle for survival in such heart-rending and desolate conditions would entail.

Britain gives up all her nuclear weapons. Britain is dependent on A for vital supplies of oil. B has nuclear weapons and threatens to take control of A.

Britain tries to interfere but B threatens to bombard her with nuclear weapons. Britain is at the mercy of the country with nuclear weapons.

Questions

1. a What is the difference between an atomic bomb and a hydrogen bomb?
   b What is special about the effects of a nuclear weapon that makes it different from an ordinary bomb?
   c What do the following initials mean? (i) ICBM; (ii) SLBM; (iii) MIRV.
   d Why was the atomic bomb first developed and why was it first used?
   e Why do you think the Cuban Missile Crisis was important?
   f What do the following words and initials mean: (i) 'superpowers'; (ii) NATO; (iii) 'deterrence'.
   g What is 'proliferation'? Why is it dangerous?
   h What do the following words and initials mean? (i) SALT; (ii) 'détente'; (iii) CND.
   i What do you think is meant by the phrase 'better to be Red than dead'?
   j Describe what you think life would be like for any survivors of a nuclear war.

2. Write an essay or hold a class discussion on the arguments for and against Britain giving up her nuclear weapons.

3. Read the following passages and answer the questions.

   ‘ Moreover, whatever promises might have been given in peace, no alliance possessing nuclear weapons could be counted on to accept major non-nuclear defeat and conquest without using its nuclear power. Non-nuclear war between East and West is by far the likeliest road to nuclear war.

   In essence we seek to ensure that, whatever military aggression or political bullying a future Soviet leader might contemplate, he could not foresee any likely situation in which the West would be left with no realistic alternative to surrender.

   To make provision for having practical courses of action available in nuclear war (or for reducing its devastation in some degree by modest civil defence precautions) is not in the least to have a "war-fighting strategy", or to plan for nuclear war as something expected or probable. It is, on the contrary, a necessary path to deterrence, to rendering nuclear war as improbable as we humanly can. ’

   Ministry of Defence Leaflet (1982)

   ‘ Three months before his death, Lord Louis Mountbatten spoke at Strasbourg about the nuclear war, and his words reflect the long experience of a great military strategist. He said:

   "As a military man who has given half a century of active service, I say in all sincerity that the nuclear arms race has no military purpose. Wars cannot be fought with nuclear weapons."

   He also said: "I can see no use for any nuclear weapons which would not end in escalation (*i.e. becoming much worse*) with consequences that no one can conceive . . . I cannot imagine a situation in which nuclear weapons would be used as battlefield weapons without the conflagration (*i.e. fighting*) spreading."

   He offered this positive alternative. "To begin with, we are most likely to preserve the peace if there is a military balance of strength between East and West . . . by reduction of nuclear armaments, I believe it should be possible to achieve greater security at a lower level of military confrontation (*i.e. fewer weapons*)." ’

   Speech by Lord Mountbatten (1979)

   a In what ways does the Ministry of Defence explain that Britain supports NATO's nuclear strategy?
   b Explain the differences in attitude towards nuclear weapons of the Ministry of Defence and the late Lord Mountbatten.

'The Guardian', 2 September 1982

4. Look at the cartoon above and answer the questions.
   a What is the meaning of the symbol held by the squire representing Europe?
   b Who are the two 'knights'?
   c Why are the two knights shown as being puzzled about the squire's behaviour?

5. Study the cartoon on p. 21 and answer the questions.
   a In what year did the USA have the greatest lead over Russia in nuclear warheads?
   b Compare the production of nuclear weapons by America and Russia from 1975 to 1981.

3 Ways of keeping peace

Treaties throughout the years: Emperor Napoleon and Tsar Alexander meet on a raft at Tilsit, 1807; Prince Bismarck presides over the congress of Berlin, 1878; Treaty between Germany and Russia at the end of the First World War signed at Brest-Litovsk, 1918

3.1 The problem of keeping peace

Various ways

International law and treaties

Inside each country police forces and armies keep law and order. The problem is how to keep law and order *between* countries.

Over the centuries various treaties have been signed by countries. All these agreements are called international law. For example, the agreement that: no nuclear weapons are stationed in space; criminals who escape to another country may often be extradited; each country has its own territorial waters.

Diplomacy

Conflict can often arise because of misunderstandings. Most countries send people to live in other countries in order to keep in touch with the foreign governments. These people are called 'diplomats'; and the most important diplomats are called 'ambassadors'. They can sometimes help to smooth out difficulties.

In recent years, as travel has become faster and easier, it has become much more common for senior politicians themselves (that is, Prime Ministers and Presidents) to meet for discussions.

Deterrence

Most countries want to be able to defend themselves against attacks. A country which has peaceful intentions will hope to deter aggression, that is, make an enemy too afraid to attack (see p. 21). One way to deter aggression is for a country to build up powerful armed forces. Another way is for several countries to sign a treaty to agree to help each other if attacked.

Public opinion

It is sometimes felt that if ordinary people really want peace, they should persuade their governments to behave in peaceful ways. So ordinary people occasionally demonstrate against what they believe to be their government's warlike policies. In recent years movements have been organized to protest against nuclear weapons (see pp. 26–27). Also, to promote peace and so that different nations can understand each other better, cultural and sporting events are arranged between countries.

Some recent efforts to keep peace

Treaties

The traditional way of showing that countries will be friendly towards each other is by signing treaties. This is still used. Here are two examples:

1 'Ostpolitik'. This is German for 'eastern policy'. After the Second World War Germany was split into two – a Communist East Germany and a non-Communist West Germany. For many years some politicians in West Germany dreamed of reuniting them. This might have meant West Germany taking over East Germany and angering Russia. From 1973 to 1975 the Chancellor of West Germany signed treaties saying that East Germany had a right to exist as a separate country.

2 American friendship with China. The Communists gained control of China in 1949. For many years after, the Americans and Chinese disliked each other very much. In fact, in the Korean War from 1950 to 1953 they even fought each other. However, in 1972 the American President visited Peking and signed a treaty of friendship.

'Shuttle diplomacy'

Some politicians, American especially, have tried to cope with crises by flying many thousands of miles to talk to the various people involved and to try to organize a settlement. In the 1970s Henry Kissinger became famous for this 'shuttle diplomacy' (as it was called)

An embassy building: entrance to the British Legation in Peking, c 1900

The problem of keeping peace

Mr Eban, Israeli Foreign Minister, welcomes Dr Kissinger on a visit, 1973

in the Middle East. During the Falklands crisis between Britain and Argentina (see p. 11), Alexander Haig tried the same method.

Contact between statesmen

1 *Reasons.* It is often felt that diplomats do not really have enough authority to arrange agreements. Peace therefore really depends on the top politicians – the Prime Ministers and Presidents – understanding each other, avoiding conflict and making agreements. Today's fast methods of travel and communication (see pp. 123–129) have made it possible for these people to be in close contact.

2 *'Hot-line'.* After the fright of the Cuban Missile Crisis (see p. 18) a teleprinter link was set up to keep the American and Russian leaders in touch in the event of another such serious crisis.

3 *Great Power 'Summit' Conferences.* During the Second

President Nixon accompanied by Chinese Prime Minister Chou En-lai, Peking, 1972

The problem of keeping peace

Bulganin (USSR), Eisenhower (USA), Faure (France) and Eden (UK) at the Geneva Summit Conference in 1955

Begin, Sadat, Carter (waving L to R) during the Camp David talks, 1978

World War the three main Allied leaders, Roosevelt, Stalin and Churchill, met several times. Churchill believed that these meetings were vital. So, after the war when there were quarrels between Russia and the western countries, he suggested similar meetings. These were called 'Summit Conferences' because they were attended by the 'highest' people. Two were held, in 1955 and 1960, but were not successful.

4 *Other crisis 'Summit' Meetings.* Several international crises have been resolved by gathering together leading statesmen from other countries. One of the most famous occasions was Camp David in 1978. American, Egyptian and Israeli leaders met in the USA and the wars between Egypt and Israel were brought to an end.

5 *Regular 'Summit' Meetings.* Several groups of statesmen now arrange regular meetings to ensure as much agreement as possible. Some of the most important are:
a) the European Community;
b) the Commonwealth;
c) the Non-Aligned Countries (i.e. neither pro-American nor Communist).

6 *Economic 'Summits'.* World economic problems have in recent years worried leaders of the rich western countries. They met for example at Cancun in Mexico in 1981 to discuss 'North-South' problems (see chapter 7). Also the finance ministers of the western industrialized countries meet each year.

Nuclear Disarmament
See pp. 24–27.

United Nations
See the rest of this chapter.

3.2 The United Nations (UN)

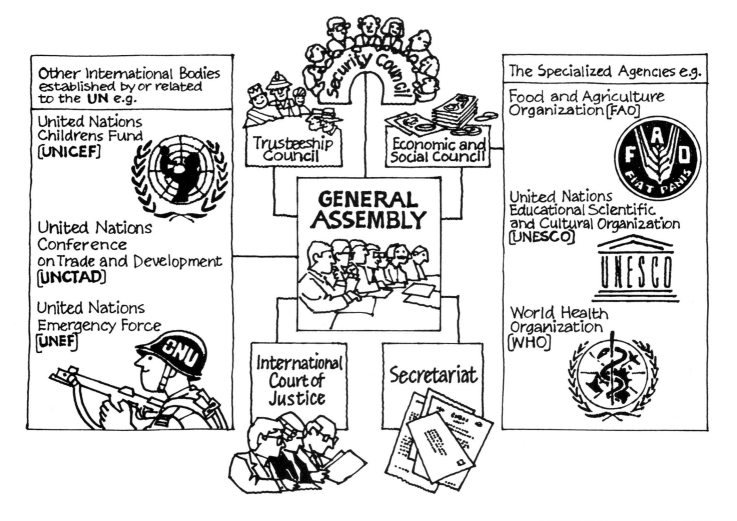

UN buildings

In an area of New York city known as Turtle Bay stands a great slab of a skyscraper. It is the main building of the United Nations Organization and completely dominates the other buildings on the 17-acre UN site. It is sometimes thought that this is the only UN building. In fact, the organization is very complicated and widespread. It has important offices in several other cities such as Geneva, Paris, Rome, Vienna, and Washington.

The United Nations (UN)

Some United Nations buildings: Headquarters, New York (above); Palais des Nations (originally League of Nations) Geneva (bottom p. 34); UNESCO, Paris (top right); FAO, Rome (right)

Origin of the UN

The basic idea

How did such an organization come into being? After most of the great wars in modern history, politicians have gathered together to arrange peace treaties. But rarely did these arrangements last long before war once again shattered the peace, especially in Europe.

So the idea developed that politicians, and their advisers, should be able to meet at any time to settle quarrels peacefully – not just at the end of a war. The first time that this idea was tried seriously was after the First World War, when the League of Nations was created.

The outbreak of the Second World War showed that the League

The Opera House, San Francisco, where the UN was founded

The United Nations (UN)

had been a dismal failure. Nevertheless, the Allied politicians, particularly President Roosevelt of the USA, did not despair. Rather they were determined to do better when their war came to an end.

The founding of the UN (1945)

And so it came about that the founding conference for the new United Nations Organization was opened on 25 April 1945 in the great Opera House in San Francisco. After much haggling and bitter disagreements a set of rules was agreed. This was called the 'UN Charter'. It was signed by the representatives of 51 countries – the founder-members.

The UN 'family'

The introduction to the UN Charter shows that the new organization set itself a formidable range of tasks. There were four main aims:

‘   WE THE PEOPLES OF THE UNITED NATIONS DETERMINED
to save succeeding generations from the scourge of war, which twice in our lifetime has brought untold sorrow to mankind, and

to reaffirm faith in fundamental human rights, in the dignity and worth of the human person, in the equal rights of men and women and of nations large and small, and

to establish conditions under which justice and respect for the obligations arising from treaties and other sources of international law can be maintained, and

to promote social progress and better standards of life in larger freedom.   ’

These aims could only be realized if a large number of bodies were set up, with specialist as well as central directing committees. The chart on page 34 shows just how complicated this great collection (or UN 'family' as it is sometimes called) has become. We cannot do more here than discuss the work of a few of these bodies.

(*Above*) *The United Nations General Assembly in session*

(*Left*) *The United Nations flag*

3.3 The General Assembly

Members

The General Assembly is a large body set up by the UN for general discussion.

Who are members?

The UN Charter declares that all 'peace-loving states' may be members of the UN. Although the UN has come in for much criticism, almost every country has chosen to become a member when the opportunity has been presented. (Switzerland remained outside the Organization, keeping to her policy of being a completely neutral country.) By 1984 there were 159 member-countries.

Change in membership

The increase from 51 to 159 member-countries from 1945 to 1984 has changed the general character of the UN considerably. In particular, it has changed the General Assembly, where all countries are represented. In the early days the members were either the most powerful countries of the world or those which were strongly influenced by them. For example, the countries of Eastern Europe tended to side with the USSR, and those of Central and South America with the USA. And the USA could almost always bank on getting its way in the Assembly. Today, however, the majority of members are the poorer countries of Asia and Africa. They are particularly keen to use the UN to put to rights the injustice of their poverty.

Importance

Speeches

But does the General Assembly actually *do* anything? It has very little real power for taking action. And it has often been criticized for being a group of people who hardly even listen when their fellow members are making their set speeches. Yet speeches are made on all the important world problems, and in this way issues are brought to the attention of people who might themselves have the power to act.

An example

In November 1974 Yasser Arafat was invited to speak to the Assembly. Arafat has been the Chairman of the Palestinian Liberation Organization. The Palestinians lost their own land when Israel was created in Palestine in 1948 (see pp. 42 and 73). This occasion at the Assembly was important because the UN treated Arafat as if he were a head of state (someone such as a President of a republic or the King or Queen of a monarchy). In other words, they recognized that the Palestinians had a right to a country of their own. Arafat made the moment dramatic: he spoke of his desire for peace but showed that he was an Arab freedom-fighter by speaking in Arabic, wearing the traditional *kefiyyah* headgear and a pistol-holster.

Informal discussions

More important than the set speeches are the opportunities provided for informal talking. Because almost every country is represented, people from any combination of countries can get together to talk over and ease their differences.

Yasser Arafat, Chairman of the PLO, at the UN General Assembly, in 1974: 'I have come bearing an olive branch and a freedom fighter's gun. Do not let the olive branch fall from my hand'. The Israeli delegation boycotted the meeting (empty seats, left)

3.4 The Security Council

The UN Security Council voting about the American invasion of Grenada, 1983. The mural is a Norwegian painting symbolizing mankind emerging from suffering

Members

The General Assembly is a large body for general discussion. The Security Council is responsible for tackling threats to peace and is a much smaller committee. It consists of representatives from 15 countries. They and their advisers sit round a horseshoe-shaped table to try to resolve disputes or to listen to complaints.

   1 Five countries are permanently represented on the Council: the USA, the USSR, China, Britain and France. These were the most important and powerful countries when the UN was set up in 1945.

   2 The other countries take it in turn to be represented, ten at a time.

Importance

The veto

One of the biggest problems relating to the Security Council concerns the veto. It is fairly obvious that if any of the powerful countries objects strongly to a proposed UN action, it would in practice be almost impossible to carry it out.

   Therefore it was thought it would be realistic to give the permanent members of the Council the power of veto. That is, any one of the 'big five' can prevent a decision it dislikes by voting against it. In the early days Russia felt that the UN was controlled by America so that she, Russia, could never muster a majority of friendly countries. Her

representatives on the Security Council therefore constantly used the veto – so much so, in fact, that they came near to wrecking the work of the Council.

Weaknesses and strengths

The veto has been a weakness. So also has the fact that the Security Council has no military force of its own to enforce its decisions. Is it, then, of any value? It has in fact arranged some useful peace-keeping operations (see pp. 40–43). In addition, it is the only truly international body for bargaining over and trying to settle disputes.

3.5 The Secretary-General

1 **Trygve Lie (1946–53)**, *a blunt, energetic, working-class Norwegian*

2 **Dag Hammarskjöld (1953–61)**, *a brilliant, cultured Swedish diplomat*

3 **U Thant (1961–71)**, *a calm patient Burmese Buddhist*

Five Secretaries-General

The person with the job of seeing that the decisions of the Security Council are carried out is the Secretary-General. Five men have held this position since 1946. U Thant and Waldheim served two five-year terms; Lie resigned because of criticisms and Hammarskjöld died in office.

4 **Kurt Waldheim (1971–81)**, *a determined and ambitious Austrian diplomat*

5 **Javier Perez de Cuellar (1981–)**, *a quiet, scholarly and discreet Peruvian diplomat*

Powers of the Secretary-General

Limited authority

To try to keep the peace in a world of constantly quarrelling countries seems a rather thankless task. No wonder that Trygve Lie described the post as 'the most impossible job in the world'! Originally it was even intended that he should have no real powers of his own – he was merely to put into practice the decisions of the Security Council. However, Article 99 of the UN Charter states:

‘ The Secretary-General may bring to the attention of the Security Council any matter which in his opinion may threaten the maintenance of international peace and security. ’

This article has been used by Secretaries-General to prod the UN into activity in certain crises.

Can anyone be impartial?

However, if the Secretary-General is to be more than a passive servant, can he be relied upon always to act in an impartial way?

By far and away the most forceful Secretary-General was Dag Hammarskjöld. He used Article 99 to get the UN involved in the terrible troubles of the Congo (see p. 41). The Russians objected to the way Hammarskjöld behaved in this crisis and Khrushchev made a protest in the General Assembly. Khrushchev believed that no individual *could* be impartial. So he suggested that the post of Secretary-General should be filled by three people – one from the Western countries, one from the Communist countries and one from the Third World.

The powers, personality and impartiality of the Secretary-General are, indeed, crucial questions. There are times when it is inefficient or

The Secretary-General

even impossible for groups of people to act. There are times when it must be an individual who makes a decision, gives a judgment or issues an instruction. In the UN that individual must obviously be the Secretary-General. It is therefore vital that he be a person who is completely trusted by all countries. Such a person is, of course, very difficult to find. And in any case, many governments do not wish to have the UN interfering in their quarrels! They therefore do not like the prospect of a powerful and determined personality like Hammarskjöld in the post.

Perez de Cuellar

The present Secretary-General, Perez de Cuellar, was chosen after a great deal of squabbling behind the scenes. He was 62 when he was appointed and had had very valuable experience both as a diplomat for his own country, Peru, and in service with the United Nations in various lands. Also, he has a reputation for being extra careful and sensitive in negotiations. It is said that if you asked him the time of day, he would give you only an off-the-record answer!

Soon after becoming Secretary-General, Perez de Cuellar was faced with the quarrel between Britain and Argentina over the Falkland Islands in the South Atlantic. However, although he worked extremely hard for a solution, he could not prevent the war between the two countries. By 1985 he was struggling to persuade the Greek and Turkish leaders in Cyprus to reach a peaceful solution to their quarrels.

3.6 Peace-keeping operations

What is peace-keeping?

When the United Nations acts to try to prevent or stop violence, it can use two main methods. It can send armed soldiers to act as 'policemen' to keep the opponents separated or to stop them killing each other. Or else it can send unarmed observers to report on any breach of the peace.

The soldiers are provided by various members of the UN on the basis of their willingness to help and their impartiality in the crisis. When they are working for the United Nations the soldiers wear light-blue berets or helmets – the UN colour. They have difficult and often dangerous tasks. They must try to prevent or stop fighting without themselves fighting: even the armed soldiers are usually ordered to shoot only in self-defence.

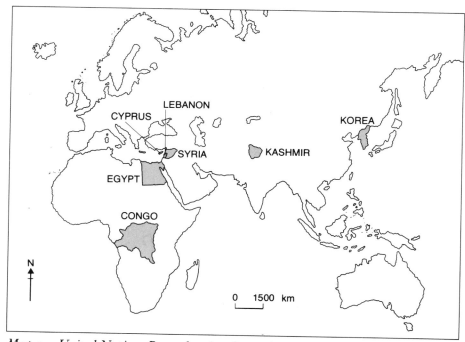

Map 1 United Nations Peace-keeping Operations

Map 1 shows the places where UN peace-keeping operations have been carried out. Here are descriptions of events in just two areas.

Peace-keeping operations

The Congo

The problem

The central African country now known as Zaïre used to be called the Congo and was for many years a Belgian colony. It is a huge country – nearly a million square miles, the size of Western Europe. The climate is humid, there is much tropical rain forest and few roads and railways.

In 1960 the Belgians suddenly gave the country independence. They had not trained the Congolese to run their own country; the people were divided into a number of rival tribal groups; and many Europeans and Americans wanted to keep control of Katanga, a province extremely rich in minerals. As a result, when the Belgians left, the country was thrown into chaos.

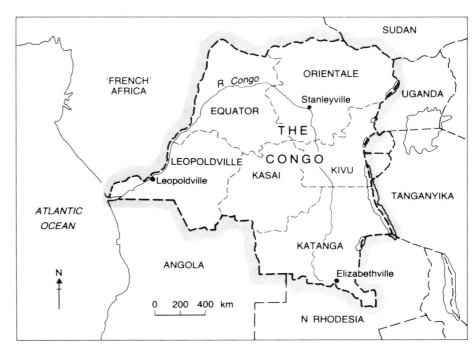

Map 2   The Congo Crisis

The UN Operation

The Congolese government appealed to the UN for help. Apart from the Korean war (1950–53) the Congo operation was to prove the biggest and most difficult of all UN peace-keeping operations. It lasted four years. Soldiers were sent by several countries. They had to restore and keep law and order. They also had to prevent Katanga from splitting away and becoming a separate country under Western control. A number of civilian experts were also sent to keep essential services running and to train the Congolese to run them themselves.

Dag Hammarskjöld was Secretary-General when the crisis blew up. He felt that this was exactly the kind of problem that should be solved by the UN. He became personally very involved. However, the way he handled matters displeased the Russians and Khrushchev expressed his displeasure at the General Assembly.

Hammarskjöld even went to the Congo himself to try to help. Soon after he arrived he flew to a meeting with Congolese leaders. His aeroplane crashed and he was killed. The cause of the crash has never been discovered.

UN peace-keeping force in Leopoldville, the Congo, 1960. The letters on the helmets stand for the French 'Organisation des Nations Unies'

Peace-keeping operations

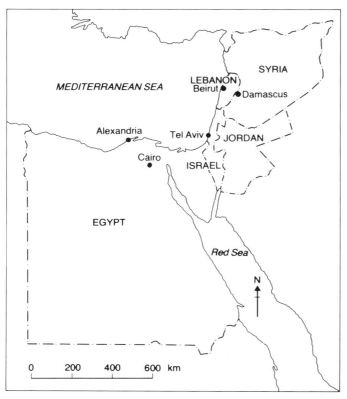

Map 3   The Middle East

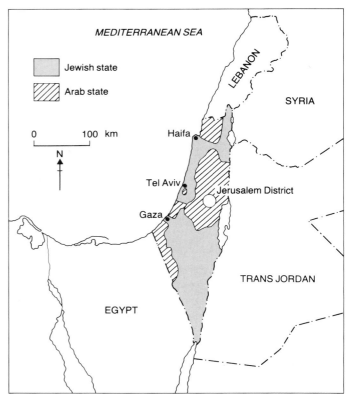

Map 4   United Nations partition plan for Palestine, 1947

The Middle East

The partition of Palestine

Since 1945 the Middle East has been the most dangerous area of continuous and complicated conflict in the world. The UN has been called upon to send several peace-keeping forces.

Until 1948 the Jewish people had had no country of their own since ancient times when they had lived in Palestine. During the Second World War the Jews in Europe suffered unbelievable horrors. Nearly six million were slaughtered in the Nazi death-camps. It was therefore agreed after the war that the Jews should have their own country of Israel again in Palestine. The problem has been, however, that the land of Palestine had been inhabited for centuries by Arab people. For 30 years until 1948 Britain governed

Palestine. But the problem of resolving the rights of the Jews and the Palestinians was so difficult that Britain asked the UN to handle it.

The UN produced a plan to partition Palestine into Jewish and Arab parts. But when the new country of Israel came into existence war immediately broke out between it and its neighbouring Arab countries. For neither Israel nor the Arabs really liked the partition scheme, though no one could think of a better solution. Eventually the UN called a truce. The Swedish Count Bernadotte was appointed in charge of military observers to make sure that fighting did not break out again. But he was murdered on 17 September 1948, the first victim in a UN peace-keeping operation.

Count Bernadotte, UN mediator in Palestine

UNEF (United Nations Emergency Force)

The Middle East was the scene of another crisis in 1956. In that year Britain, France and Israel attacked Egypt because of a quarrel they had with President Nasser. However, the three invading countries agreed to

Peace-keeping operations

withdraw their soldiers when a UN force was arranged for the area. This force (UNEF) was placed on Egyptian soil along the frontier with Israel. But it was withdrawn when war broke out again between Egypt and Israel in 1967.

UNDOF (United Nations Disengagement Observation Force)

War broke out yet again in 1973 – this time between Israel on the one side, and Egypt and Syria on the other. As the fighting came to an end UN forces (UNDOF) were sent to act as 'buffers' between the Israeli and Egyptian soldiers in Sinai, and the Israeli and Syrian soldiers in Syria.

UNIFIL (United Nations International Force in Lebanon)

One of the smallest countries in the Middle East is Lebanon. Although it is small, it has a very mixed population, and several groups, especially the Christians and Muslims, are rivals. Also many Palestinian refugees have been living there. Since 1976 the Lebanon has

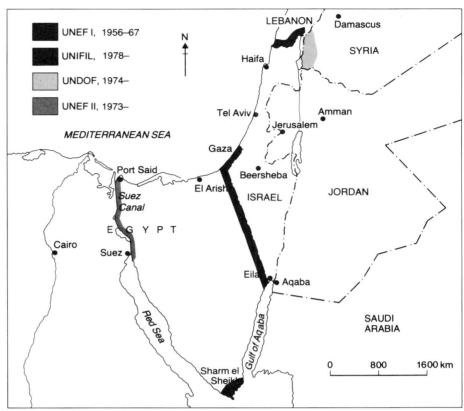

Map 5   United Nations peace keeping operations in the Middle East

been torn by civil war and there have been constant clashes across the frontier between Israelis and Palestinians. In 1978 a UN force (UNIFIL) was sent to the southern

Lebanon to try to reduce the violence. This was swept aside in the invasion by Israel in 1982, becoming important again when Israeli forces withdrew in 1985.

3.7 Social and economic work of the UN

Range of work

Importance

The political and military events in which the UN is involved, especially the really dramatic ones, like those we have been describing, are the ones which hit the headlines. Yet many people believe that the best achievements of the UN have been in its social and economic work. Since 1945 a great deal has been done to improve co-operation between countries in a vast number

of ways. The chart on p. 34 shows a few of the great array of organizations which work through the UN's Economic and Social Council. For it is recognized that the world will never be a truly peaceful place if the sourges of human misery and poverty are ignored.

The different kinds

We can divide this work very approximately into five main kinds:

1 *Smooth running of services*: for example the Universal Postal Union;

the International Civil Aviation Organization.

2 *Conferences on world problems*: such as Human Environment (Stockholm, 1972) – leading to the United Nations Environment Programme; World Food (Rome, 1974) – leading to the World Food Council.

3 *Help for those in distress*: for example the High Commissioner for Refugees; the Disaster Relief Co-ordinator.

Social and economic work of the UN

Bangladeshis learning fish-farming techniques at Kwangchow in China, 1978, in a training scheme arranged by the UN Food and Agricultural Organization (FAO)

4 *Improving trade and prosperity*: such as the General Agreement on Tariffs and Trade (GATT) (see p. 114); the World Bank (see p. 113); the United Nations Conference on Trade and Development (UNCTAD) (see p. 115).

5 *Technical assistance*: for example the World Health Organization (WHO); the Food and Agriculture Organization (FAO). Both WHO and FAO have important achievements for the poorer countries of the world to their credit. Great progress has been made in checking serious diseases such as smallpox, cholera and malaria. Also the development of fast-growing crops and the introduction of irrigation schemes have improved food supplies.

6 *Educational cultural and scientific work*: for example UNESCO (the United Nations Educational, Scientific and Cultural Organization).

An example – UNICEF

It is not possible, of course, to outline here all the work done by all these bodies. Here is just one example.

UNICEF, the United Nations

(International) Children's (Emergency) Fund, exists to help the world's children, many millions of whom suffer from poverty and ill health. One of its main tasks is to try to prevent malnutrition. Many children in poor countries suffer

A UNICEF diary sold to raise money for children in poor countries

Social and economic work of the UN

either from lack of food or lack of a properly balanced diet. Terrible diseases and death often result from malnutrition.

Thousands of UNICEF experts work throughout the world. They teach mothers how to feed their children as best they can with the local food. They distribute free food for children through health centres and schools. They train local people to look after young children. Many people in the rich countries of the world think that this kind of work is worthwhile – that children should be helped because they cannot help themselves. And so UNICEF is able to raise money by voluntary contributions. Very successful schemes are the sale of calendars and Christmas cards.

A medical team working for the World Health Organization (WHO) in Kabul, Afghanistan. The doctor is taking a mouth-swab from a child

3.8 Conclusion

Weaknesses of the UN

The United Nations is often bitterly criticized. Its officials are inefficient and waste a lot of money. Since it has been in existence the world has become a much more dangerous place – scores of wars have been fought and thousands of nuclear weapons have been made. The UN has been powerless to stop all the violence. Nor does it seem capable of doing anything effective to ease the dire strains on our planet – of poverty, over-population, environmental decay (see chapter 10).

Importance of the UN

Would the world, then, be any the worse if the UN did not exist? Yes, it would – for four main reasons:

1 The day to day social and economic work of the UN has brought much benefit to millions of people. Although the USA provides the bulk of the money for UN work, it is doubtful if it or any other country would undertake this kind of work directly itself.

2 The countries of the world are today haphazardly linked together much more closely than ever before in history. Communications by aeroplane, radio, telephone and trading across the seas have made this so. Representatives of the various countries of the world therefore need to be meeting constantly to try to ensure that the systems work as smoothly as possible.

3 The UN exists to provide ways and means for the countries of the world to co-operate if they want to do so. It was never intended to be a world government.

4 Relations between countries are very complicated. If peace is to be preserved and extended, all the varieties of methods for negotiation and collaboration must be used.

Questions

1
  a What title is given to the most important diplomats?

  b What is meant by 'shuttle diplomacy'?

  c When and where was the UN founded?

  d Explain in your own words the four main aims of the UN.

  e In what ways do you think the General Assembly is important?

  f What does Article 99 of the UN Charter state? Why do you think it is important?

  g Who have been Secretaries-General of the UN since 1971?

  h Do you think the UN peace-keeping operations in the Middle East have been of any use?

  i What do the following initials mean?
(i) WHO; (ii) FAO; (iii) UNCTAD; (iv) UNESCO; (v) UNICEF.

  j How has the UN been able to help ordinary people?

2 Write an essay or hold a class discussion on the idea of a world government and how it might work.

3 Look at the cartoon below. What do you think the cartoonist meant to represent by: (a) Noah; (b) the Ark; (c) the animals; (d) the doves; (e) the water.

'*Punch*', *14 December 1960*

4 Some of the most useful and practical international work is that which tackles hunger and disease. Many official and voluntary bodies undertake this work, such as UNICEF, Oxfam, Christian Aid. Select one of these organizations, find out as much as you can about it and write a report on its work.

5 Read the following passage and answer the questions.

> ❝ THE chief argument in favour of World Government is that, if suitably constituted (*i.e. organized*), it can prevent war. It would, however, be quite easy to construct a supranational (*i.e. controlling all individual countries*) organization which might be *called* a World Government, but would not effectively prevent war. Such a Government would encounter much less opposition than one in which all serious armed force was under the command of the World Government.
>
> Much the strongest objections arise from the sentiment of nationalism. When we say, 'Britons never, never shall be slaves', our hearts swell with pride. The feeling in favour of national freedom is one which has been rapidly increasing throughout the last hundred and fifty years, and, if World Government is to be inaugurated (*i.e. started*), it will have to take account of this sentiment and do whatever is possible to satisfy it. ❞

Bertrand Russell, *Has Man a Future?* (1961)

  a What is the difference, in the author's view, between 'World Government' and a 'supranational organization'? (paragraph 1).

  b What is the main objection to a World Government? (paragraph 2).

6 Organize a mock United Nations meeting. Help to arrange this may be obtained from:
The Council for Education in World Citizenship,
19–21 Tudor Street,
London EC4Y 0JD
(Tel: 01-353 3353.)

4 The challenge of Communism

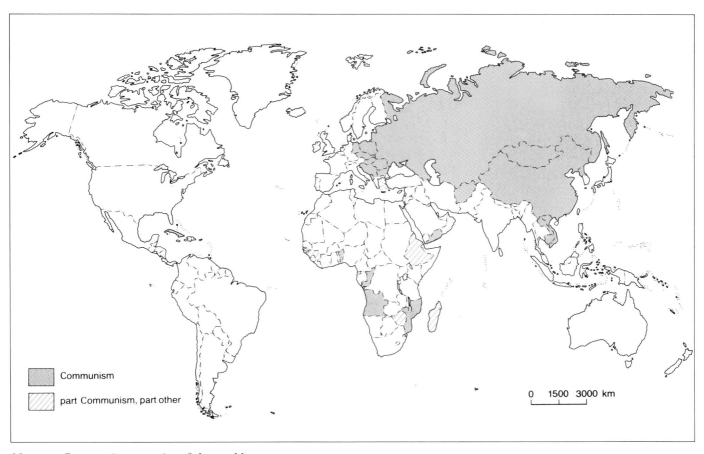

Map 1   Communist countries of the world

4.1 Communism throughout the world

Which countries are Communist?

Roughly half the people in the world are living in countries with governments that could be labelled Communist. It is necessary to say 'could be' because the countries shown on the map are so different and are governed in such different ways. They nevertheless share certain basic beliefs and ways of running their governments.

In addition to the countries with Communist governments there are several countries which have important Communist Parties, though not strong enough to be part of the government. Communist Parties are particularly important in India, Italy and France.

The importance of history

Since Communism is so widespread in the world, it is important to understand what it stands for and why it is so strong.

However, it is difficult to understand what Communism stands for today without first studying its history. This is because present-day communists are trying to put into practice the theories of the great thinkers of the past. People who hold these beliefs are often called Marxists or Leninists or Trotskyites or Maoists, after the men who wrote about these theories.

The Chinese leader Hua Guofeng at the tomb of Marx, in Highgate, London 1979

Life and work of Karl Marx

The idea of equality

The basic idea of Communism is equality. There are in the world today wide differences in wealth, between the fabulously rich and the wretchedly poor. The point of view that such differences are unjust is not in fact new. But in the nineteenth century certain writers started to think especially seriously about the problem – to wonder how this inequality had come about and how matters could be changed. By far and away the most important of these writers was Karl Marx.

Marx's life (1818–1881)

Marx was born in 1818 in what is now Germany. He had a brilliant mind and no doubt could have enjoyed a comfortable career in law or government. Instead he chose a hard life, devoting himself to study and trying to put the world to rights. He became involved in revolutionary movements in the 1840s, was hounded out of several continental

The main ideas of Marx and Engels

Marx and Engels believed that the world is steadily progressing so that eventually all people will be treated equally. They believed that this progress is happening in the following way:

1 Class differences.

Ever since primitive times people have been divided into different classes. One class has been rich and powerful; another has been poor and downtrodden.

By the nineteenth century, when Marx and Engels were writing, the two main classes in European countries were the bourgeois and the proletariat. Bourgeois are rich people (sometimes also called capitalists) like owners of factories and banks. They own most of the country's property such as houses. They also control the governments. The proletariat are people who work in towns like factory-workers.

2 Revolution.

The bourgeois will become richer and the proletariat will become poorer. The proletariat will become so miserable and discontented that they will rise up in revolt. Street demonstrations and fighting in the towns will lead to the overthrow of the government. This is called a revolution. The bourgeois will have their wealth and power taken from them.

3 Communism.

These revolutions will happen in the countries with most industry and therefore the most discontented working people. Gradually these revolutions will spread throughout the world. There will then no longer be any class differences. Under this new Communist system all people will work honestly and in return receive what they need for a comfortable life. The slogan is:

FROM EACH ACCORDING TO HIS ABILITY; TO EACH ACCORDING TO HIS NEEDS.

The origins of Communism: Marxism

countries and finally settled in England.

He lived for most of the rest of his life in cramped and squalid rooms in London. He died in 1881. His tomb in Highgate cemetery is to this day a place of pilgrimage for those who follow his teachings.

The Communist Manifesto, 1848

Marx had one particularly close friend. This was Friedrich Engels. Engels in fact helped out the Marx family with gifts of money. In 1848 the two men together wrote the most famous of all Communist books, *The Communist Manifesto*. It ends with the following famous words:

‘ Let the ruling classes tremble at a Communist revolution. The proletarians have nothing to lose but their chains. They have a world to win.

Working men of all countries, unite! ’

This photograph, taken in 1864, shows Marx (holding hat) with his three daughters (Jenny, Eleanor and Laura) and Engels

4.3 The Russian Revolution: Leninism and Trotskyism

This propagandist painting shows Lenin addressing a group of fighters in the Russian Revolution. Stalin (hand in coat) stands to his right and Trotsky (leaning on the table) is behind him

The Russian Revolution: Leninism and Trotskyism

In fact, the first Communist Revolution did not take place in a heavily industrialized country, as Marx and Engels predicted. It happened in Russia, quite a backward country compared with the USA and Western Europe. Nor were there successful revolutions in other countries immediately after. The Russian Revolution broke out in 1917 and Russia remained the only Communist country for nearly 30 years.

The two most important leaders of the Revolution were Lenin and Trotsky. Besides organizing the Revolution, they added extra ideas about how Communism would spread.

Lenin (1870–1924)

Lenin's work

Lenin was born in 1870 and spent most of his adult life plotting revolution. He spent many years before 1917 outside Russia in order to escape from the Tsar's secret police. He created the Bolshevik Party, which was pledged to stir up revolution in Russia as soon as possible. He also started a newspaper, *Pravda* ('Truth') (see photograph right). After the Revolution Lenin took control of the government and started turning Russia (now also called the Soviet Union) into a Communist country.

Lenin's theories

Marx and Engels had been rather vague on two matters. They did not explain how the perfect, Communist way of life could in practice be set up after the Revolution. Nor did they take much notice of the wealth that countries like Britain were gaining from colonies in Africa and Asia. Lenin filled these gaps in the following ways:

1 Party.

He believed that the working-class people could not organize a revolution and a Communist society themselves - they don't have the necessary skills and exprience. A small group of trained and dedicated people need to do all this on behalf of the workers. This group is the Communist Party. There must also be a period of transition between the Revolution and the final, full Communist system. During this time the Party would rule.

2 Imperialism.

In the nineteenth century and the first half of the twentieth century several European countries had empires in various parts of the world. Lenin believed that these countries obtained cheap food and raw materials from their colonies. The working people of those European countries therefore enjoyed cheap food and clothes at the expense of the poor colonial people who produced them for only starvation wages. So the European workers were less discontented than Marx and Engels had expected. Lenin therefore believed that revolutions would need to take place in the colonies first before they could be expected to happen in countries like Britain and France.

Lenin at his desk, 1918. He is reading 'Pravda', the newspaper he started. It is still the official newspaper of the Communist Party in Russia

The Russian Revolution: Leninism and Trotskyism

Trotsky (1879–1940)

Trotsky's work

Lenin was the political planner and organizer of the Revolution in Russia. His right-hand man was Trotsky, who was the military genius.

He organized the take-over of key places, like the telephone exchange in the capital, Petrograd (now named Leningrad). Immediately after the Bolsheviks (or Communists) took over control of the government, their opponents tried to fight back. There was a civil war. The Communists were eventually successful largely because their army, called the Red Army, was commanded so skilfully by Trotsky.

Trotsky's theories

Like Lenin, Trotsky also was concerned that the Revolution had started in Russia rather than a more fully industrialized country. He therefore produced his theory of 'the permanent revolution'. He believed that until revolutions happened in the advanced industrial countries, they would be a threat to Russia. The only way of making sure that Communism really succeeded was for the Russian Communists to concentrate on stirring up revolutions in those countries even before completing the reforms in Russia itself.

Three leaders of the Russian Revolution: Joseph Stalin, Vladimir Lenin, Leon Trotsky

4.4 Totalitarianism: Stalinism, Maoism, the Khmer Rouge

Stalin (1879–1953)

Stalin takes control

Lenin did not enjoy robust health. He died in 1924, aged only 54. It might be thought that Trotsky was the obvious man to succeed him as head of the Russian government. In fact a man named Stalin, who had not been so important during the Revolution, gained control.

Trotsky and Stalin became bitter rivals. Trotsky had to flee Russia and eventually settled in Mexico. He

Stalin

defended himself in a house which he turned into a small fortress. But eventually one of Stalin's secret agents managed to strike up a friendship with him. When they were alone one day in 1940, the agent smashed Trotsky's skull with an ice-pick he had smuggled in in his coat pocket.

Why did Stalin feel that he had to destroy the man who had been his rival so many years before? The reason was partly that Stalin completely disagreed with Trotsky's

Totalitarianism: Stalinism, Maoism, the Khmer Rouge

idea of permanent revolution. Stalin believed that he should concentrate on building up the strength of Russia first before trying to spread Communism elsewhere.

The other part of the reason was that Stalin would not allow anyone to stand in his way. He produced plans for the growth of Russian industry at break-neck speed. The development of Russian industry and armed forces over the past 60 years has been truly remarkable. It was Stalin who laid the foundations of Russia's present industrial and military strength – by a great expansion in key industries such as coal-mining, steel production and the generation of electricity.

Stalin and those who helped him took over *total* control of the whole of life – even what kind of pictures artists should paint. This kind of government is called 'totalitarian'.

Russia under Stalin

Russia was plunged into misery:

1 The richer peasants were forced to give up the private ownership of their land. Agriculture was thrown into chaos. Millions died of starvation.

2 Large numbers of peasants were forced to move to towns to become workers in the new factories.

3 A great army of secret police was organized to hunt down opponents. Millions were sent to labour camps in the wastelands of Siberia and the Arctic. Many died in these bitter conditions. Many more were executed.

4 When Stalin wanted to get rid of politicians, he forced them to confess in public to the most incredible charges of treason and spying before having them shot.

Mao Tse-tung (1893–1976)

Could peasants produce a Revolution?

While Stalin was ruling as dictator in Russia, Communists were organizing themselves for eventually taking control in China. Their leader was Mao Tse-tung. A long civil war was fought until in 1949 Mao was able to take control of the country.

Even more so than Russia, China has the great majority of its people working on the land as peasants. So China seemed an even less likely country to have a Communist Revolution, if Marx was right about the importance of the factory workers in a revolution (see pp. 48–49). However, Mao believed that peasants could be organized into an army to overthrow the government. And he proved it! The teachings of Mao have therefore become very important for inspiring Communists in other countries in Asia and Africa to believe that they could organize successful revolutions in their countries.

Mao Tse-tung as a young man. The way of representing Chinese words, including names is now being changed. As a result Mao's name is sometimes spelt 'Mao Zedong' – nearer to the proper pronunciation

Harvest reapers meditate on Chairman Mao Tse-tung's sayings before working

Totalitarianism: Stalinism, Maoism, the Khmer Rouge

The Cultural Revolution

However, Mao also, like Stalin, tried to control the whole of life. During his last ten years he tried to force the ideas of the Great Cultural Revolution on to the Chinese people:

1 All were made to wear the same kind of tunics.

2 Many people were taken from their normal jobs and forced to work on the land or in factories. As a result, education was disrupted as teachers were taken away from schools and universities.

3 Peasants were forced to live in communes.

4 Because of the chaos and opposition many people died of starvation or were executed, though not so many people suffered as in Russia.

Kampuchea

The Khmer Rouge

The most horrifying use of mass slaughter and physical work to make all people equal happened between 1975 and 1978 in Kampuchea.

This is a small country, once called Cambodia, in South-East Asia. First of all the Americans tried to stop Communists taking control of South-East Asia. They caused dreadful death and destruction by bombing the country. Then a fanatical group of Communists called the Khmer Rouge took control. They forced people to leave the cities and work on the land. All normal trading stopped. People were ill-treated and killed quite indiscriminately.

The agony of Kampuchea

Here is one eye-witness account:

‘ Here and there we could see the bodies of villagers who had been killed by the Khmer Rouge, presumably because they didn't want to leave their homes.

On 19 April, at 10 in the morning, I saw the Khmer Rouge arrest about twenty young men with long hair; they shot them before our eyes. Everybody was terrified and had their hair cut at once, even in the middle of the night. ’

In 1970 the population of the country was about eight million. The Khmer Rouge boasted that 'one or two million young people are enough to make the new Kampuchea!'

Balance sheet

Debit and credit

It is very difficult to discover very accurately how many people were executed or died of starvation, disease or brutal treatment in Russia, China and Kampuchea. Fifty million all told is perhaps a reasonable estimate. It is a horrifying figure.

Life in Russia and China is now returning to something like normal and no doubt soon will in Kampuchea. The ordinary working people in Russia and China are today living far happier and healthier lives than their grandparents.

Important questions

But were these dreadful sacrifices necessary to achieve these improvements? And if they were necessary, can the slaughter of past generations be justified for the welfare of the present?

And, a final set of questions. Are the horrors of totalitarian government an inescapable part of Communism? Or are they perversions of true Communism? Would events have turned out more happily if the revolutions had taken place in industrialized countries, as Marx predicted?

There is little doubt that Karl Marx would have been horrified if he had risen from his grave in Highgate and witnessed the terrible deeds that have been perpetrated over the past generation in his name.

Evidence of slaughter in Kampuchea. It is estimated that in five years nearly half the population died in fighting, from famine or as a result of the political killings

4.5 Communism with a human face

How East Europeans have disliked Russians

Yugoslavia

In the years immediately following the Second World War Communist governments were set up in many countries of Eastern Europe, but very much under the control of the Russians. However, the leader in Yugoslavia, Marshal Tito, refused to be ordered about by Stalin and a freer system than the Russian gradually developed there. One of the most important features of the Yugoslav system is the way workers are allowed to help in the running of their own factories.

Uprisings against Russia

Many people in other East European countries disliked the strict government forced upon them by the Russians. The Russians introduced:
1 secret police;
2 government control of trade unions;
3 censorship of newspapers.
There have been several uprisings of angry people to try to set up freer forms of government. The most important were in:
1 Hungary in 1956;
2 Czechoslovakia in 1968;
3 Poland in 1980.
The Russians crushed the uprisings in Hungary and Czechoslovakia with the use of tanks. In Poland a free trade union, called 'Solidarity', was set up – the first to be formed in a Communist country. But the government and the army arrested its leaders.

More freedom

Even so, life is much freer in Russia and Eastern Europe than it was during Stalin's last years (he died in 1953). By the early 1980s Hungary had probably become the freest country as a result of very gradual reforms after the 1956 crisis. Even inside Russia itself people were starting to criticize the government and demand reforms. It is true that they run the risk of being put in prison (or a mental asylum – the favourite modern method!). But the complaints still get heard.

Western Europe

Eurocommunism

The Russian action in Hungary and Czechoslovakia shocked many Communists in Western Europe. In the 1970s the leaders of the Communist Parties in France, Italy and Spain started to insist that they were quite independent of Russia.

Also they promised that, if voted into the government, they would co-operate with other parties in their parliaments for the reforms they wanted. In other words, they would not try to bring about a bloody, violent revolution. These new ideas have come to be called 'Eurocommunism'.

Britain

Members of the Communist Party of Great Britain have often stood for election to Parliament. But no candidate has sat in the House of Commons since 1950. Communists are more successful in gaining influential positions in several important trade unions.

Inside the Labour Party, too, there are a number of people who accept the theories of Marx and even some who follow the ideas of Trotsky. The most extreme are called the 'Militant Tendency'.

Lech Walesa (pronounced 'vah-wensa', second from left) at the port of Gdansk in Poland, where the Solidarity trade union movement started

4.6 Communism in the Third World

Why is Communism popular in the Third World?

Poverty

As we shall see in chapter 7 hundreds of millions of people in Africa, Asia and Latin America are extremely poor. If there are also rich people (see p. 93) or rich companies in these countries, the poor resent the differences and want a fairer sharing out of wealth. For the poor, Communism is a means of ending this inequality.

Foreign control

This resentment is especially strong if the rich are foreigners. European countries no longer rule large areas of the world as colonies. However, European and especially American companies have great influence over the economies of some of these poor countries. Some Third World countries have felt that this foreign economic control has been so serious that their countries are still not truly free. They have called this economic control 'neo-colonialism'.

The most famous example of this control of poor countries' economies has been in Central America. Here the United States United Fruit Company has so controlled plantations and canning factories that these small countries have been called 'banana republics'.

We have already seen (p. 50) that Lenin wrote about the evils of imperialism. The poor countries therefore see Communism as a way of ending this foreign exploitation.

Cuba

Cuban Revolution

We saw on pages 3 and 4 how the hated government in Cuba was overthrown in 1959. The leader of the new government was Fidel Castro. He soon quarrelled with the USA because he nationalized some of the most important United States controlled parts of the Cuban economy. The Americans even supported an unsuccessful invasion of Cuba in 1961 to try to overthrow Castro. Soon Castro became a Communist and asked Russia for help.

Cuban help to others

In recent years Cuba has helped a number of Communist movements in both Latin America and Africa. You can see from map 2 (below) which countries Cuban forces have been involved with. Cuban soldiers have fought in Angola, Ethiopia and Grenada, for example. Weapons have been supplied to the Communist Government in Nicaragua and to rebels fighting against the American-backed Government in El Salvador.

Spread of Communism in the Third World

Some people, especially in the USA, believe that the Russians and Cubans are plotting to spread Communism throughout the Third World against the wishes of the peoples of these countries.

Others believe that where Communists have gained control of governments, they have been supported by the people because of the problems we have noted above.

Map 1 (p. 47) shows which countries have become Communist. However, there are many differences between these governments; and they are not necessarily controlled in their policies by Russia or Cuba.

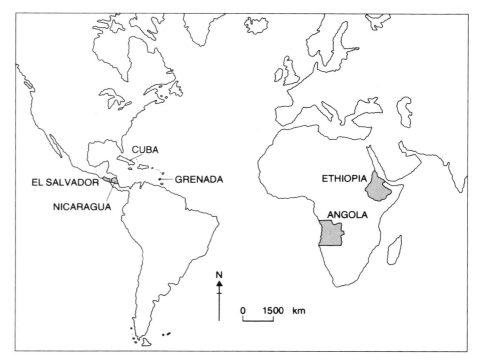

Map 2   Countries where Cuban forces have been in recent years

4.7 The Cold War

Communist countries v. Capitalist countries

Marx believed that there were two rival classes in industrial countries (see p. 48): the middle-class (bourgeois) and the working-class (proletariat). In the world today there are also rival groups of countries, magnifying this class rivalry.

Communist countries like Russia believe that they represent the working class and that America and her friends represent the middle class. The Communists believe that this rivalry will continue until all countries eventually become Communist.

For many years the communist leaders believed that this rivalry would eventually break out into all out war. However, since the development of nuclear weapons (see chapter 2), it has been generally agreed that war would be suicidal.

Russia v. America

Tension between them

The rivalry between America and her friends, or 'allies', and Russia and hers since the end of the Second World War has been called 'The Cold War'. In other words, America and Russia have not been involved in a 'hot', shooting war with each other.

But they *have* been unfriendly towards each other in many different ways.

They have even been involved in 'hot' wars in other countries to protect their control over various parts of the world. Both sides have arranged great military alliances with their allies (see map 3):

1 The American alliance is called the *North Atlantic Treaty Organization* (NATO).

2 The Russian alliance is called the *Warsaw Pact*.

The only part of the world where these forces face each other across a shared frontier is in Germany.

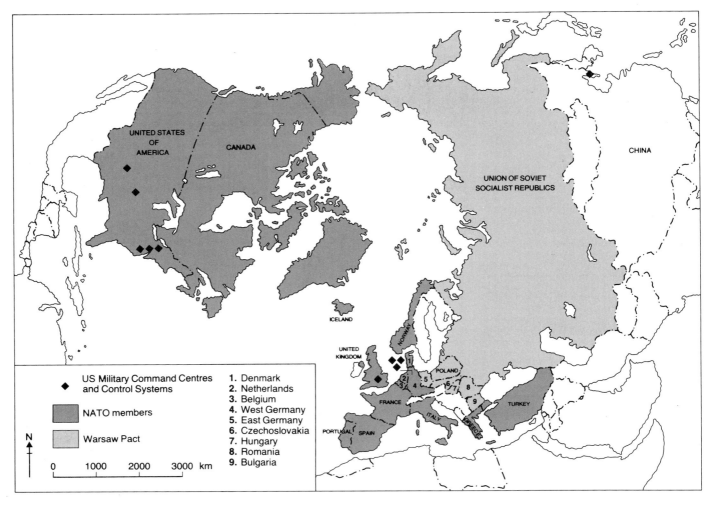

Map 3 Cold War confrontation between NATO and the Warsaw Pact

The Cold War

Why are they frightened of each other?

Each side is frightened of the other. The Americans are afraid that the Russians will help to set up Communist governments in even more countries. For example, it is unlikely that Communist governments would be in control in much of Eastern Europe today if the Russians had not forced them on the people in the late 1940s. On the other hand, the Russians do not influence all Communist governments. For instance, there have been very serious quarrels between Russia and China for many years.

But just as the Americans are frightened of the Russians, so the Russians are as frightened of the Americans. Russia and her allies seem to be surrounded by the armies, navies and air forces of the Americans and their allies. Also the Americans seem just as guilty as the Russians of supporting unpopular

governments in other countries – in their case, in Central and South America particularly. Yet if the Communists believe that their system is destined to spread throughout the whole world, perhaps the Americans are very wise to build up these defences?

Sometimes Communist countries quarrel with each other. This photograph shows Russians (in white) clashing with Chinese frontier guards on the River Ussuri, 1969

4.8 The balance of arguments

How to decide?

It is difficult to present the arguments for and against Communism entirely fairly. There are able and sincere people on both sides who think that their side is right and the other is evil.

The arguments are therefore often carried on with a great deal of emotion. It is often a matter of trying to balance the various advantages and disadvantages on either side. It is not possible to *prove* that one side is better than the other. Each individual must make up his/her own mind. Here are some important points to consider when trying to decide.

American military advisers (background) helping government troops in El Salvador, Central America

The balance of arguments

In favour of Communism

It preaches equality

Many people suffer from poverty and injustice. Some others have a worried conscience or feel angry about this poverty and injustice. The teachings of Marx give these people hope for a better world, an ideal to work for.

It is intended to benefit everyone

The Western economic system is called capitalism. It is based on the idea of making a profit. Owners of factories and shops, for example, will employ their work-force, pay wages, invest in new buildings and machinery only with a view to making a profit. The economy should surely be *planned* for the benefit of the people as a whole, not the profit of a few. The failure of the capitalist system is shown by the problems of inflation and unemployment in recent years (see pp. 109–111).

Many benefit in following generations

Systems of government have been set up to make sure that these profits can be made. For example, many people have suffered imprisonment and torture in countries in South and Central America in recent years. The USA has helped to keep these governments in power because US firms make so much profit in these places. It is true that some people have suffered because of Communist revolutions. But violence is necessary to break the hold of a powerful, tyrannical government. Many more people in the generations that follow in fact benefit.

It is anti-colonial

Many of the countries of Asia and Africa have been colonies. Capitalists make great profits from trade with these colonies. Even now that these colonies have become independent countries, western companies still benefit from trade with them. This is one reason why most of the countries of Africa and Asia remain very poor (see chapter 7).

The balance of arguments

Against Communism

It is an atheist belief

Marx said that 'Religion is the opium of the masses'. In other words, religion is a set of myths used by the ruling class to persuade the lower classes to accept their lot in this world. The Christian churches have been persecuted in several Communist countries, particularly Russia and China.

Many people in western countries, especially the United States, believe that Christianity is an essential part of their way of life. Many people in the Middle East believe that Islam is an essential part of their way of life (see chapter 5). These people therefore insist that Communism must not be allowed to spread to their countries.

It has not worked in practice

A planned economy sounds very good in theory. Surely it makes sense for the government to decide how many of what goods should be produced to meet the needs of the people. In fact, planning has not

worked in Communist countries.

The most notorious example is Russian agriculture. In spite of the vast size of the country, it cannot grow enough food to feed its people. Large quantities of grain have to be bought from America each year.

The clue to the problem is human nature. The story is told of a western journalist being taken on a tour of a Russian factory by the Russian Prime Minister, Khrushchev. 'How many men work in this factory?' asked the journalist. 'About half', Khrushchev replied with a sad grin. If you are not allowed to keep at least some of the profit from your own work, why make the effort?

People lose their freedom

We have seen above (p. 53) how great numbers of people have died under Communist governments. Political freedom is very restricted in many of these countries. No other political parties, apart from the Communist Party, are allowed. Trade unions are completely controlled by the government. The newspapers and broadcasting are

The balance of arguments

censored so that no one can criticize the government. Surely the freedoms enjoyed in western countries are too precious to give up?

Communism is developing its own empire

The colonies of the great European Empires in the Americas, Africa and Asia have become independent. But the Russians too have had a great Empire – the vast lands of northern Asia. Yet these non-Russian peoples have not been given their independence. Many are Mongol or Turk in race, Muslim in religion. In fact, the population of the Asiatic provinces are growing so fast that the Russians themselves will soon be in a minority.

Also Russian soldiers at various times have prevented the people of East Germany, Hungary, Czechoslovakia and Afghanistan from managing their own affairs.

Convergence

In any case, some people believe that the industrialized Communist and Capitalist countries are becoming increasingly like each other.

In many western countries class differences have become very blurred and the government runs some industries (by nationalization) and provides a basic standard of life (the Welfare State). In some Communist countries it is now permissible to make a private profit.

Perhaps Karl Marx's prediction that the two systems will move further apart will not happen?

In Communist countries the official churches are 'registered'. But many Christians in Russia find too much government interference and restriction in these, so unregistered groups of believers meet secretly, often in woods as here

Russian cartoon reproduced in 'The Observer', 23 March 1960

Questions

1.
  a. Why was Karl Marx so important?
  b. What is a social class?
  c. How did Marx think a revolution would happen?
  d. What is the difference between Marxism and Leninism?
  e. What do the following mean?
     (a) totalitarian;
     (b) Cultural Revolution.
  f. What is 'Solidarity'?
  g. What is 'Eurocommunism'?
  h. Who is the head of the Government of Cuba?
  i. Why is Communism popular in the Third World?
  j. What does the phrase 'Cold War' mean?
  k. What is NATO? What is the Warsaw Pact?
  l. What are the arguments for and against a planned economy?

2. Study the following extract from the Manifesto of the British Communist Party and answer the questions.

❝ In Britain, as in other capitalist countries, a deep seated crisis of the whole economic, political and social system affects adversely every aspect of life. The wealth, effort and ingenuity which should be used to improve the lives of the people are used instead to enrich the few and wasted in war preparations. A handful of great monopolies and banks dominate the country. . . . The rate of exploitation increases and the gap between rich and poor grows wider.

It has never been so clear that capitalism is an outdated system, unable to use the vast scientific advances to benefit the people. The new techniques and discoveries which could, in the right hands, end insecurity and poverty for all time, are misused to increase private profits and to prepare ever more devastating wars.

The Communist Party believes that a new social system is needed, for the present one is increasingly failing. The working people will have to make a revolutionary change, end capitalism and build a socialist society. Only then, when the people own the means of production and decide their own destiny, will the miracles of modern science perform miracles for the welfare of the great majority. ❞

  a. Why, according to the Communist Party, are the British people not enjoying life as much as they might?
  b. What do the following words mean?
     (i) 'monopolies';
     (ii) 'capitalism';
     (iii) 'means of production'.

3. Read the following song and answer the questions. (From George Orwell's book *Animal Farm*:

a 'fairy story' written as a comment on Communism.)

Beasts of England, beasts of Ireland,
Beasts of every land and clime,
Hearken to my joyful tidings
Of the golden future time.

Soon or late the day is coming,
Tyrant Man shall be o'erthrown,
And the fruitful fields of England
Shall be trod by beasts alone.

Rings shall vanish from our noses,
And the harness from our back,
Bit and spur shall rust forever,
Cruel whips no more shall crack.

Riches more than mind can picture,
Wheat and barley, oats and hay,
Clover, beans, and mangel-wurzels
Shall be ours upon that day.

Bright will shine the fields of England,
Purer shall its waters be,
Sweeter yet shall blow its breezes
On the day that sets us free.

For that day we all must labour,
Though we die before it break;
Cows and horses, geese and turkeys,
All must toil for freedom's sake.

Beasts of England, beasts of Ireland,
Beasts of every land and clime,
Hearken well and spread my tidings
Of the golden future time.

  a. Who do you think the 'Beasts' represent?
  b. Who is 'Tyrant Man'?
  c. What do the animals hope for? What does this song tell us about the hopes of people involved in a Communist Revolution?
  d. Do you think the author, George Orwell, was *for* or *against* Communism?

4. Write an essay or hold a class discussion on whether the disadvantages of Capitalism can be changed without a revolution

5. Study the cartoon on p. 60. The Russian politicians are being greeted and handed bouquets from rows of people. Why are they shown as blocks of concrete? Why do you think the cartoonist had to go in to hiding to escape from the secret police?

5 The political power of religion

Pope John Paul II blesses the crowd who thronged to the holy shrine at Czestochowa in the Pope's native land of Poland

5.1 Religion and politics

What is religion?

Could you define the word 'religion'? Most religions teach that there is a God or there are gods. These gods are believed to have supernatural powers beyond any powers that human beings have. However, by striving to follow the teachings of these gods, man can improve himself, can come nearer to perfection. Many people in the world today believe that there is no truth in any of the religions. These people are called 'atheists'. However, many millions of people throughout the world still hold to their religions.

How do religion and politics mix?

Reasons for the connection

It is often felt that religion and politics should be kept quite separate: politics is about life in the present; religion is about the life hereafter. Jesus Christ once said, 'give to Caesar what is Caesar's, and to God what is God's.'

In fact, however, it is often impossible to keep them separated. There are two main reasons for this:

1 *Violence.* Some deeply religious people hold their beliefs quite fanatically. They believe that people with other religions (or with none) are evil or are dangerous to them. Throughout history and still today people have killed each other for religion. Very often religious

violence is due to fear. People of one religion fight another because they are afraid of what might happen to them if the others gain control. However, governments are responsible for keeping law and order and for protecting their own people. So governments have become involved in religious conflicts.

2 *Laws.* Although religions teach about matters of the spirit, they also teach about good behaviour on this earth. Governments therefore sometimes pass laws to support religious beliefs. For example, adultery is a crime in some Muslim countries.

Sometimes religion leads people to disobey their government. For example, in the First World War some men were sent to prison

Religion and politics

Map 1   The main religions of the world

because they were conscientious objectors. That is, because of their religious beliefs they refused to join the army to kill other human beings.

In many countries it would be impossible to become a political leader unless you belonged to a particular religion. It would be impossible, for instance, for anyone who was not a Christian to gain enough votes to become President of the United States. In Britain it is actually laid down that the Queen (or King) must be a Protestant Christian. Sometimes even religious leaders become political leaders. The most recent example has been in Iran with the Ayatollah Khomeini.

Religion as a human bond

Religion can, indeed, be a great bond. A people who share a deeply held religious belief can make heroic sacrifices and achieve great things. For example, Stalin, the Russian leader, believed that only armies counted. He once asked 'How many divisions (of soldiers) has the Pope?' And yet when the German armies were penetrating deep into Russia during the Second World War, Stalin was glad to reopen the Christian Churches he had closed down. For he realized that the people needed their Christian faith to defend their motherland.

Queen Elizabeth II, attended by the Archbishop of Canterbury, at her coronation

5.2 Christianity

Christianity throughout the world

The Christian religion and churches developed from the teachings and work of Jesus Christ and his disciples, who lived in the Middle East nearly two thousand years ago. Christians believe Jesus is the 'Messiah', the promised deliverer of the Jews. Jews are still waiting for the Messiah to come (see p. 72).

There are now three main branches of Christianity in different countries. They are:

Orthodox – Russia, Greece, Cyprus.

Protestant – Northern Europe, North America, South Africa, Australasia.

Catholic – Central and South America, southern Europe, Poland, Ireland.

In the colonies in Africa and Asia European missionaries have converted many people to Christianity. Christianity is now therefore often felt to be connected with the way the Europeans controlled these colonies. So it is sometimes disliked.

Also some black people in the USA have felt that Christianity is the religion of the white man. And so they have become Muslims (see p. 84).

However, the most serious deliberate attacks on Christianity have taken place in Communist countries. After all, Communists believe that Marxism explains the whole of man's life. They cannot therefore allow a rival belief to exist. On the other hand, the Catholic Church remains extremely important, for example in Poland. There the church holds the loyalty of the people so well that the government does not dare to take action against it.

Papal Swiss Guard standing in the Vatican, 1958, while the Cardinals are in Conclave to choose a new Pope. They elected John XXIII

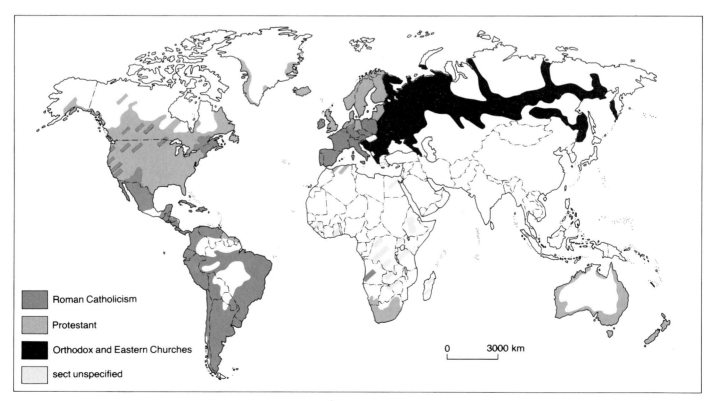

Roman Catholicism

Protestant

Orthodox and Eastern Churches

sect unspecified

0   3000 km

Map 2   Christianity throughout the world

Christianity

The Catholic Church

The Papacy

The Roman Catholic Church has held the faith and loyalty of its members more effectively than the Protestant or Orthodox branches.

Perhaps one of the reasons for this is the fact that, wherever they live, Roman Catholics have a recognized leader. This is the Pope.

The senior priests in the Catholic Church are called Cardinals. When a Pope dies they meet together to choose one of themselves as the new Pope. Popes live in their own tiny independent city called Vatican City in Rome. Most Popes have, in fact, been Italians.

Recent Popes

One of the most famous Popes in recent years was John XXIII. Generally speaking the Catholic Church tends to dislike change. It is often accused of failing to move with the times. Pope John made a great effort to adapt to modern times and to persuade people throughout the world (not just Catholics) how dangerous international quarrels can be in an age of nuclear weapons. Although he reigned for only five years, he was admired by very many people.

In 1978 a very different man was elected as Pope – John Paul II. Most Popes tend to be quite old by the time they are elected (John XXIII was 76). John Paul II was only 58. A second difference is that he is not Italian, but Polish. Thirdly, he has stopped the trend of bringing the Catholic Church more into line with modern ways of life. He strongly believes that it is his duty to uphold traditional values, especially of family life.

More than any other Pope he has travelled to many countries. He has often been greeted by great throngs of welcoming people – an indication of the continuing faith and loyalty of millions of Catholics.

Pope John Paul II crossing Westminster Bridge in his 'Popemobile', designed for his protection against assassination attempts

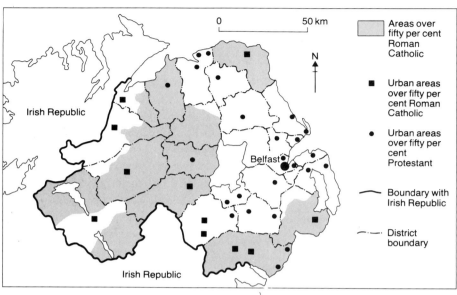

Map 3   Northern Ireland: religious divisions

Map legend:
- Areas over fifty per cent Roman Catholic
- Urban areas over fifty per cent Roman Catholic
- Urban areas over fifty per cent Protestant
- Boundary with Irish Republic
- District boundary

Historical background

Protestants and Catholics

Christianity teaches that all men are brothers. So it is a sad distortion of the faith when Christians fight and kill each other *because* of their religion. This is what has been happening in Northern Ireland in recent years.

In order to understand the unhappy condition of Northern Ireland we need to delve back a little into history.

Five hundred years ago most people in Western Europe were Christians and accepted the Pope as head of the Christian Church. Then, in the sixteenth century, some people became dissatisfied with the Pope and the way the Church was run. As a result, Protestant Churches were set up. This was known as the 'Reformation'.

For many years Catholics (who still followed the Pope) and Protestants hated each other. In wars and civil wars many atrocities were committed. These kept the hatred alive. However, by the twentieth century Protestants and Catholics in the majority of countries have come to live with each other in perfectly friendly ways.

Ireland under English control

But matters are very different in Ireland. In the sixteenth century England became a Protestant country; Ireland remained Catholic. To make matters worse England has treated Ireland cruelly ever since the Middle Ages – by conquest and keeping the Irish people in dire poverty.

In the seventeenth century, Protestant people settled as colonists in the northern part of Ireland called Ulster. At the end of that century King James II tried to make England Catholic again. This plan was so unpopular he had to flee from England in 1688.

A Dutch Protestant, William of Orange, then became King of

Members of the Protestant Orange Order on their traditional parade through Belfast

Northern Ireland

England. James then went to Ireland where he was, of course, supported by the Catholic people. He went to Ulster to try to defeat the Protestants there and besieged the city of Londonderry. King William landed with an army and defeated James at the Battle of the Boyne in July 1689.

King William remains a great hero of the Protestants of Northern Ireland to this day. Those who feel particularly strongly are called 'Orangemen'. The anniversary of the Battle of the Boyne is celebrated every year.

Ireland partitioned

At the end of the nineteenth century England decided that Ireland should be allowed to be independent. But the Protestant people in Ulster were naturally frightened of what might happen to them. After all, there are many more Catholics than Protestants in Ireland as a whole. It was therefore arranged that Ireland should be divided. Ulster stayed part of the United Kingdom: Southern Ireland became independent. This happened in 1921. But the boundary was drawn in such a way that the province of Northern Ireland which stayed in the United Kingdom included many Roman Catholics, although the majority were Protestants.

Because the Protestants are the majority they have been able to take control of the local government and police, take for themselves the best jobs and best houses. The Catholics thought the whole arrangement unjust. A secret, private army was created in 1921 to try to reunite the whole of Ireland. This is the Irish Republican Army (IRA). In 1969 the Catholics in Northern Ireland started to demonstrate for better conditions. There has been violence there ever since.

This bitter cartoon about the British legacy in Ireland appeared in 'The Sunday Times' in 1971

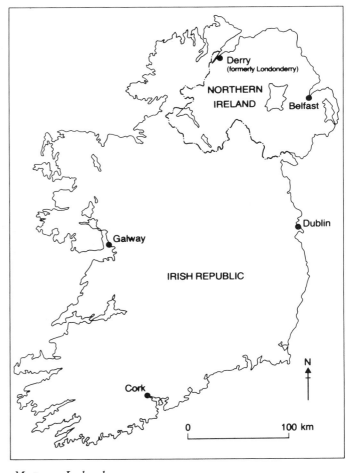

Map 4   Ireland

Northern Ireland

'The Troubles'

Complicated problems

Why do you think it is so difficult to restore peace in Northern Ireland?

The local police could not cope with all the bombings and shootings. So English soldiers were sent to keep law and order. The position then became complicated:

1 Catholics kill Protestants;

2 Protestants kill Catholics;

3 but in addition the Catholic IRA now kill English soldiers and even English civilians in England, because they represent English control over Northern Ireland.

The problem seems to have become impossible:

1 The Catholic Irish Nationalists will accept nothing less than a united Ireland. Their soldiers, the IRA, kill quite mercilessly to try to force the English government to agree to this (see pp. 5 and 7).

2 The Protestant Northern Ireland Loyalists or Unionists, as they are called, want to remain loyal to and united with England for their own protection.

The IRA bomb attack on a cavalry parade, Hyde Park, London, 1983

Revd. Ian Paisley, the Unionist leader, speaking to supporters in Belfast

Ian Paisley

The fears of the Protestants have been emphasized by one of their leaders, the Revd. Ian Paisley.

In his writings and speeches he uses extreme language to stir up religious emotion. Here are some examples of the way he refers to Roman Catholics:

‘ I have hated God's enemies with a perfect hate. ’

‘ The forces of popery are the scarlet whore drunk on the blood of the churches. ’

‘ They are devotees of that godless monster which has drenched Ireland with blood for many generations – the godless monster of a united Ireland. ’

5.4 Islam

The Islamic religion

Three great religions, each sharing many of the same beliefs and traditions, have developed in the Middle East. Christianity is one of them. The other two are Judaism and Islam.

Muhammad

Islam, the religion of Muslims, was founded by Muhammad about 1400 years ago. He lived in what is now Saudi Arabia. Much of his life was spent in Mecca, which as a result became the holy city of the Muslims.

Muslims, like Christians and Jews, believe that there is only one God. Muslims call their God 'Allah'. They believe that God has had several prophets who have persuaded people to believe in Him. They believe Moses was one, Jesus Christ was another, but that the greatest prophet has been the Prophet Muhammad.

For the sake of modesty Muslim women traditionally wear a 'chadour' to cover their bodies and faces

Muslim pilgrims arriving at the holy city of Mecca for joyous festivities

The Koran

Just as Christians have the Bible as their holy book, so Muslims have the Koran as theirs. However, the Koran gives rules about the conduct of life in much more detail for example:

‘ You are forbidden the flesh of animals that die a natural death, blood, and pig's meat. ’

‘ As for the man or woman who is guilty of theft, cut off their hands to punish them for their crimes. ’

When some Muslim countries today try to live by the Koran, they sometimes appear harsh and out of date to people in Western countries. Adultery, theft, drinking alcohol, for example, are all very severely punished. On the other hand, Muslims think that people in the West are wickedly lax about these matters.

Islamic countries

The spread of Islam

In the same way that Christianity spread from its original home, so did Islam. Saudi Arabia is the birthplace of Islam. But today the majority of people in countries of northern Africa and western and south-east Asia are Muslims.

The governments and laws of some are strictly guided by religion; such as in Libya, Saudi Arabia, Iran and Pakistan. The rulers of Libya and Iran have emphasized their belief in Islam because they dislike the West so much. Pakistan separated from India in 1947 for religious reasons (see p. 71).

Muslim extremists

Some of the most extreme Muslims believe they should convert or even kill 'infidels' (those who do not belong to the Islamic faith). Some say that a holy war, or 'jihad' (p. 76),

Islam

should be fought for this purpose. This is how Islam spread so quickly in the Middle Ages. Recently Muslims have not been so warlike.

In some countries, especially Egypt, there is an organization called the Muslim Brotherhood. The most extreme members are willing to use violence to try to bring about ways of life strictly in accordance with the Koran. Because Anwar Sadat, the President of Egypt in the 1970s, made a peace treaty with Israel, a great enemy of the Arabs, he was killed by Muslim extremists.

Iran

However, the country that has been trying to live most strictly according to Islamic rules is Iran.

For most of this century Iran has been ruled by Shahs. However, the Shah's Government became hated:

1 in the 1970s the Shah became very friendly with America;

2 his secret police arrested and cruelly tortured anyone who opposed the government.

When a revolution broke out and the Shah had to flee abroad the new ruler of Iran was the religious leader, the Ayatollah Khomeini. He was 78 when he took over the Government and became very popular with the ordinary people of Iran. Local government was taken over by the local priests or mullahs. The Parliament has been controlled by the Islamic Republican Party. They have passed laws to put the rules of the Koran into practice. These have sometimes been very strictly enforced. For example, men and women found alone together have been arrested if they are not relations. Women are required to wear the modestly all-enveloping 'chadour' in public. 'Infidels' who oppose the Muslim Government have been executed.

This is a striking photograph of the moment when, on 6 October 1981, President Sadat of Egypt was killed by assassins

The Ayatollah Khomeini has stimulated enthusiastic support for his government, and for the fighting of a war with Iraq (governed by a rival Muslim sect)

5.5 India and Pakistan

The partition of India

For many years Britain governed the sub-continent of India. After the Second World War it was agreed that India should be independent. The great majority of Indians at the time were Hindu by religion. But the people in the western parts and some in Bengal, in the east, were Muslim. These Muslims were very afraid that they would be treated as inferiors when the British left. They therefore demanded that a separate Muslim country should be created in those parts where the Muslims lived. This was done. The new country was given the name Pakistan.

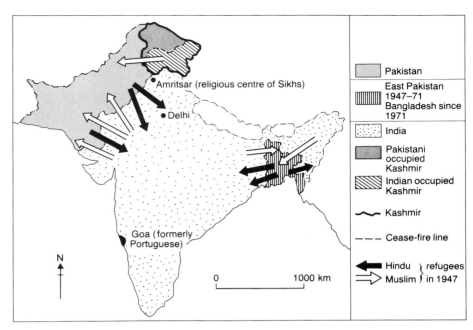

Map 5   The partition of India

Communal clashes

However, when the boundaries between India and Pakistan were drawn, many millions of Muslims found themselves to be living in India and many millions of Hindus, in Pakistan. Fighting broke out and fearful bloodshed resulted. In cities like Calcutta with mixed populations bloody clashes took place in streets.

More seriously, millions of Muslim refugees trekked into Pakistan and millions of Hindus trekked into India. At one time a great convoy of Hindus, 57 miles long, was journeying from West Punjab into India. No one knows exactly how many people moved home in this way; 10 million,

perhaps even 15 million. In the clashes homes were burned, goods stolen, people beaten, women raped and half a million or more people were killed. It was a horrifying time. India and Pakistan have remained enemies ever since. They have fought three wars.

Crowds of frightened Muslims pack this station and train in New Delhi to escape to Pakistan after bloody attacks on Muslims in 1948

5.6 Judaism

Historical background

The Jewish religion

The Jews believe that, in ancient times, through their leader Moses, they made a 'Covenant' (or agreement) with God. They call God 'Yahweh' or Jehovah. By this Covenant the Jews agreed to worship no other god but Yahweh and to follow His laws of the Ten Commandments. In return, the Jews would be favoured by God as His 'Chosen People' and be allowed to return to the Promised Land of Palestine from which they had been scattered.

Jews also believe that God is going to send them a 'Messiah', God's promised deliverer. Christians believe that Jesus was the Messiah (see p. 64). Jews are still waiting for the Messiah to come.

Wherever the Jewish people have settled they have built synagogues to worship God in, and have been taught by 'rabbis' (or teachers).

Jewish religious service in a synagogue

Jews in ancient times

The Jewish people have had a remarkable history. Their history and their religion are very closely connected. It is knowledge of this history and religion that has helped them to keep a sense of belonging together through their amazing experiences over thousands of years.

The Jewish people were constantly being taken or driven from their land of Palestine. In the first century AD there was a great rebellion against the Romans who were in control of Palestine at the time. The Romans suppressed this uprising and destroyed Jerusalem. From soon after that time very few Jews lived in their own land of Palestine. This scattering to other lands is called the 'Diaspora', (or 'Dispersal').

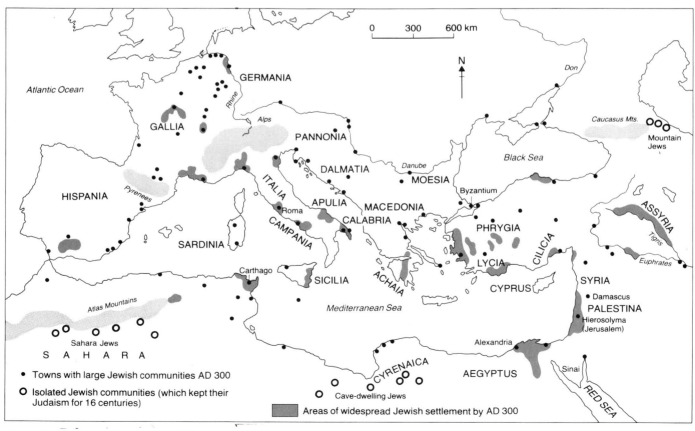

Map 6   The Jewish Diaspora (Dispersal)

Judaism

How the Jews survived

During the Middle Ages and into modern times the Jews in European countries have been persecuted, expelled, murdered (see pp. 80–81). But they never lost their sense of being Jewish:

1 They tended to live together in a particular part of a town, called a 'ghetto'.

2 Jews married Jews to help keep themselves together and in order to stay separate from Gentiles (non Jews).

3 They observed their own holy day, the Sabbath, on a Saturday.

4 They kept to strict rules for their diet: as with Muslims, the pig is believed to be an unclean animal unfit for eating: and meat can be eaten only if the animal has been prepared in a special way, that is, 'kosher'.

5 This proper way of life for the Jews is laid down in their great book of laws, the 'Talmud'.

Despite their wanderings and persecution, the Jewish people have not despaired. For they have never forgotten that they are God's Chosen People.

Israel

Zionism

The Jewish people in modern times are sometimes called 'Zion', after the name of the hill on which Jerusalem is built. Towards the end of the last century some Jews began to campaign for the return of their people to Palestine. They called themselves 'Zionists'.

The trouble was that Palestine was now inhabited by Arab people. Many politicians, especially in Britain and America, were very sympathetic to the wish of the Jewish people to have their own country. To

Map 7   Israel today

try to avoid the problem of annoying the people then living in Palestine, it was suggested that the Jews should settle in some other, more empty country. Uganda and Argentina were suggested. But, of course, the Jews would have no other than their Promised Land.

Partition of Palestine

Eventually, in 1948 a new Jewish country was created, with the name of Israel. By a plan drawn up by the United Nations, Palestine was divided into a part for the Jews and the rest to remain Arab (see p. 42). The Arabs, especially those living in Palestine, naturally objected. There has been much fighting in the area ever since. Many Palestinians have become refugees and exiles from their own country as a result.

Expansion of Israel

Even so, despite all these changes, some extremist Jews have not been satisfied with the amount of land they were given in 1948: they want all the land that had been owned by the Jews or Israelites in ancient times.

They have felt particularly strongly about two areas:

1 *Jerusalem.*   Because this city is a holy place for Jews, Christians and Muslims, the UN planned that it should be an international city. However, in the wars since 1948 Israel has taken it all.

2 *West Bank Territories.*   In 1948 the land on the west bank of the river Jordan was given to the country named Jordan. This land was captured by Israel in a war in 1967. Ever since then Jewish people have been settling there, building their own towns. It is the ambition of extremist Israeli politicians to take over this land completely. In this way they would create a Greater Israel. The reason they particularly want this land is that it was part of Judea and Samaria, important provinces of ancient Israel. In fact, politicians like Menachem Begin always referred to the West Bank territories by these names. Mr Begin was Prime Minister from 1977 to 1983 and he steadily worked for the total inclusion of this land into Isreal.

Menachem Begin in the 'Knesset' (parliament)

5.7 Non-violence

Many people would agree that suffering and violent death are evil. Religion should help people to give up evil ways. It is particularly sad that religion has so often been used as a reason or an excuse for brutality. Yet this is not always so.

Some religious leaders have used the power of religion to achieve good results in non-violent ways. The two most remarkable men in recent times to use religion in this way were Mahatma Gandhi and Martin Luther King.

Gandhi (1869–1948)

Gandhi's beliefs

Gandhi was an Indian and during his lifetime India was ruled by Britain. He believed that this was wrong and that the Indian people should be free to rule themselves. But he came to realize that to try to use force to expel the British was both impracticable and morally wrong. He was particularly interested in the gentle traditions of the Hindu and Christian religions.

Mahatma Gandhi as seen by the British cartoonist Low

His way of removing the British was by 'satyagraha'. This word is difficult to translate. It means literally 'the force of truth'. It involves demonstrating and protesting, without using violence, in support of a cause known to be just and right. You must be willing to suffer injury and imprisonment. But your opponent will eventually give in. This is because you will wear down his will-power to crush your cause: he will come to understand that you are in the right.

Gandhi's actions

Gandhi organized huge marches. He himself undertook fasts, in other words went on hunger-strike. The Indian people supported his campaigns in millions. Faced with this determination the British Government was forced to discuss with Gandhi ways in which India could become independent.

By a dreadful twist of fate, Gandhi himself suffered a violent death. During the terrible disturbances when India was partitioned (see p. 71), he was shot by a young Hindu who disagreed with the gentle way in which he was dealing with the clashes with the Muslims.

In 1930 Gandhi led thousands in a 240-mile march to the coast to make salt in protest against the salt-tax

Non-violence

What Gandhi learned from Christianity

Gandhi drew most of his inspiration from Hinduism. However, he was also influenced by some Christian teachings. For example, in the Sermon on the Mount, he read Jesus' words:

❛ But I tell you, Do not resist an evil person. If someone strikes you on the right cheek, turn to him the other also. ❜

❛ Love your enemies, bless them that curse you, do good to them that hate you. ❜

Martin Luther King (1929–68)

Discontent of the American Blacks

In the 1950s and 1960s in America many black people were finding it difficult to 'turn the other cheek'. Compared with the white people, they lived in very poor conditions and few were able to obtain good jobs. Violent riots broke out in some of the cities with large black populations.

What did Martin Luther King do?

However, one black leader insisted on using non-violent methods. This was the Baptist preacher, the Revd. Martin Luther King. Like Gandhi he believed in the power of peaceful protest. He became the most successful leader of the Civil Rights movement. He organized huge demonstrations to persuade the government to allow black people the same rights as white people – for example, to vote in elections, to attend the same schools, to ride on the same buses. For in some parts of America at this time black people were still denied these basic rights.

Martin Luther King addressing a crowd protesting outside an all-white school. Segregated education was a particular complaint of American Blacks in the 1960s

The great value of his work was recognized outside America too: and he was awarded the Nobel Peace Prize.

And just as Gandhi lived by peace and died by violence, so too did Martin Luther King. He was shot by a murderer whose only motive seems to have been the notoriety that would attach to his name by killing such a famous man.

But the memories of Gandhi and King live on as great men who proved that so much can sometimes be achieved by peaceful means, even if the obstacles seem to lesser men to be insurmountable.

❛ . . . there comes a time when people get tired of being trampled over by the iron feet of oppression. There comes a time, my friends, when people get tired of being flung across the abyss of humiliation. . . We are here this evening because we are tired now. Now let us say that we are not advocating violence. We have overcome that. I want it to be known throughout Montgomery and throughout this nation that we are a Christian people. We believe in the teaching of Jesus. The only weapon we have in our hands this evening is the weapon of protest . . . don't let anybody make us feel that we ought to be compared in our actions with the Ku Klux Klan or with the White Citizen's Council. There will be no crosses burned at any bus stops in Montgomery. There will be no white persons pulled out of their homes and taken out on some distant road and murdered. There will be nobody among us who will stand up and defy the Constitution of this nation. We only assemble here because of our desire to see right exist. ❜

Martin Luther King, speech in Montgomery, Alabama (1955)

Questions

1 a Why is it impossible to separate religion and politics?
   b Which are the most important Roman Catholic countries?
   c How important is the Pope?
   d How has religion become a cause of conflict in Ireland?
   e How does Islam influence the lives of Muslims?
   f Why were India and Pakistan created as separate countries?
   g How important is religion to the Jewish people?
   h What is Zionism?
   i Why has religion caused so much conflict?
   j How has religion been used for peace?

2 Write essays or hold class discussions on the following topics. (You will find it useful to read chapter 4 for topic **a** and chapter 2 for topic **b**.)
   a Both Communism and religion teach that 'all men are brothers'. Is Communism therefore a religion?
   b Should Christians support the existence of nuclear weapons?

3 Read Martin-Luther King's speech on p. 75.
   a What does the word 'oppression' mean?
   b What does the word 'humiliation' mean?
   c Who are the Ku Klux Klan? (See also p. 83.)
   d What does the author mean by the phrase 'There will be no crosses burned'?
   e What does the author mean by the phrase 'stand up and defy the Constitution'?
   f Compare this passage with the quotations from the Revd. Ian Paisley on p. 68. How do you explain the differences?

4 Read these two passages and answer the questions.

‘ IF, by some perverse twist of fortune, the Middle East were to be shaped by men of the sort who killed Anwar Sadat, Arab society would plummet rapidly into an obscurantist past.

Girls would be pulled out of schools, offices, factories and armed services to be kept at home. Women would appear in public only as anonymous, black sheeted bundles. There would be no 'sexual mingling' in restaurants or other places of entertainment. Indeed, many places of entertainment – bars and cinemas first – would be closed down.

Alcohol, of course, would vanish. Television, if not banned, would fill the hours with Koranic recitation. Adulterers would be stoned to death and thieves mutilated.

And all this would be brought about by force.

Two features mark the new fanatics of the Middle East. The first is that their vision of the good life is so narrowly focused on social customs: what women wear, what people eat and drink, correct butchering, ritual ablutions. They do not seem greatly preoccupied with what we call social justice or with inequalities between rich and poor, let alone the class struggle.

The second distinguishing characteristic is their violence, their readiness to kill – and to die.

Sadat's killers knew they were committing suicide. So do the Iranian mojahadine who strap grenades to their bodies before running to embrace their targets.

What is most ominous about these revolutionaries is how widely spread they are, challenging the authorities in nearly every Middle Eastern country, and how genuinely they seem to express a certain grassroots feeling. ’

The Observer, 11 October 1981

   a What would be the effects if the 'Middle East were to be shaped' by extremists?
   b According to the writer of this article, what are the two distinguishing characteristics of 'the new fanatics of the Middle East'?
   c Why does the author think that the emergence of Muslim fanatics is ominous?

‘ The giving of alms or *zakat* was an obligation on all Muslims. The law-books later fixed their level as one fiftieth of all income in money or kind. Although *zakat* came to be regarded as a form of state income tax in the Koran, it appears as the means by which the wealthy man can show his righteousness which will be tested at the Last Judgement. *Zakat* means 'purification'. It is to be employed for the poor and the needy, and those employed to administer it, and those who are to be conciliated, slaves and captives, debtors and wayfarers (Koran ix, 60).

These four 'acts of devotion' – prayer, the payment of *zakat*, the pilgrimage and fasting during Ramadan, together with *shahada* or profession of faith – form the five Pillars of Islam.

In addition to the five Pillars, Muslims are enjoined to *jihad*, which means 'striving' or 'exerting oneself', in the Way of God. Today *jihad* is usually translated as 'holy war', although there is nothing in the word to indicate that the striving is to be to carried out by the sword or the tongue or any other method. What the Koran does say (ii, 190) is: 'And fight in the way of Allah against those who fight against you but be not aggressive. Surely Allah loves not the aggressive.' Fighting is clearly limited to fighting in defence. ’

Peter Mansfield, *The Arabs* (1978)

   a What is meant by the phrase 'The giving of alms'?
   b What is the Muslim view about giving alms?
   c What is the Muslim pilgrimage?
   d What does the word '*jihad*' mean?
   e Compare the two passages about Islam. Do you think that it is a caring religion?

6 Race relations

A man with caucasoid features from South America

A man of negroid racial type from Nigeria

An Australian aborigine with distinctive characteristics

A Chinese girl with typical Mongoloid features

6.1 What is race?

Physical differences

Many people have an over-simplified view of race. For example, could you tell which countries or races the people in the photographs on p. 77 belong to? Defining a race is in fact a very difficult and complicated business.

It is possible to use a number of different tests. Some are obvious, such as skin colour; others are not visible, such as blood group. Human beings are physically different in various ways.

One of the main reasons for this difference is that during long periods of man's evolution, groups were kept apart by geographical barriers, like oceans and mountains, and each group evolved its own characteristics.

But problems arise if one assumes that divisions between races are clear and rigid. We shall see below that scientists have tried to classify races. Yet there are wide differences between individuals even within each racial division. Even if clearer differences existed hundreds of thousands of years ago, inter-marriage has led to many mixtures.

Classification of races

Some scientists have, in fact, suggested that there are four main races in the world (see map 1).

However, there are obviously sub-divisions within each of these. So for example, both Europeans and Indians belong to the Caucasoid race, yet Indians almost always have darker skins than Europeans. By including all these sub-divisions it is possible to identify about 40 racial groupings, or 'ethnic groups' as they are strictly called.

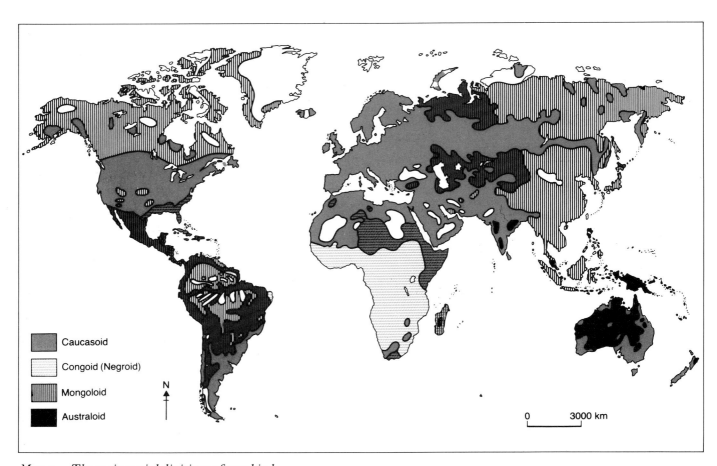

Map 1   The main racial divisions of mankind

Caucasoid
Congoid (Negroid)
Mongoloid
Australoid

N

0   3000 km

6.2 Racialism

Important words

When one person dislikes another person just because he belongs to a different race, we call this attitude 'racialism' or 'racism'. Racialism varies greatly in intensity and is, in fact, very complex. We must first of all be clear about three key words.

Prejudice

This means judging before you have the facts. Some people hold very firm opinions about what or whom they like or dislike without really knowing very much about what they are saying. People have a perfect right to have likes and dislikes. But trouble can result if they are based on rumour and not fact and especially if this prejudice leads to discrimination.

Discrimination

If people of a particular group or race are treated differently from another group or race, this is 'discrimination'. For example, a person of a particular race might be prevented from entering certain buildings or living in certain houses. Or a person of a particular race might be debarred from a particular job. Often discrimination is the action of individuals – employers, for instance. But sometimes laws have been passed to discriminate against a particular group in a country.

Stereotyping

One of the clearest kinds of prejudice is 'stereotyping'. This is when all people in a particular group are thought to have the same characteristics. For example, saying that 'all Blacks are lazy' or 'all Indians are hard-working' or 'all Jews are clever and crafty' is stereotyping. In this way individuals are not judged on their own personal merits or faults. For example, 'This

Racial prejudice and discrimination: a graffiti attack on a Bengali family's house ('Paki out' is what it reads)

man is black; all Blacks are lazy; therefore this man must be lazy' is, of course, illogical as well as being unjust and insulting. It is such labelling that is so unintelligent and harmful.

Such attitudes are reinforced by the use of abusive terms: calling Blacks 'Coons', for instance, or Jews, 'Yids'. (And people of white British origin are just as abusive towards each other: for example, Australians often refer to English people as 'Pommie bastards'.)

Causes of racialism

Dislike and prejudice can lead to mild discrimination. But it can also lead to violence – beatings, riots, even wholesale slaughter. What are the causes of racialism?

Generally speaking, human beings feel safe when they live in groups surrounded by people like themselves. They feel that 'outsiders' mean trouble – the outsiders will take their land or their jobs; or at least they will change accepted habits of life.

Sometimes racialism is just a

vague feeling of dislike among ordinary people; sometimes this feeling is stirred up to active hatred by a particular problem or by individuals wishing to cause trouble; and sometimes it is encouraged by the government.

'The Jewish Peril': a mythical plot. The cover of a racist book, c. 1934

Racialism

Ideas of 'pure' and 'superior' races

In Nazi Germany in the 1930s and 1940s these general fears became intensified when theories about racial purity were developed and put into practice. These theories started with the wrong belief that races can be clearly distinguished. Some races were thought 'better' than others. The 'best' races were thought to be those that had kept themselves as 'pure' as possible by avoiding intermarriage with other races.

If you believed that you belonged to a 'superior' race, you would tend to treat people of other races as inferior, perhaps even as almost subhuman. Some American and South African white people have treated Blacks in this way. In Asia, the Chinese feel that they are superior to other people, and in India the Indians have treated some hill tribes very badly. In the USA the white Americans slaughtered the Red Indians. The most notorious example, however, is the way the Nazis treated the Jews.

This cartoon shows a typical example of stereotyping

6.3 Anti-semitism

Are Jews a race?

Strictly speaking, Jews are not a separate race. In their original homeland they were part of what is known as the 'Semitic' racial group, which includes Arabs and is really a language group. Although Jews have lived for many centuries in other lands, some of them still have the distinguishing features of the Semitic group. And, in Nazi Germany, people were classified as Jews by how they looked. Persecution of Jews, which Christians have always been guilty of but which reached its peak under the Nazis, is known as 'anti-semitism'.

Persecution of Jews

Pogroms

For centuries the Jews in Europe lived apart from other people and followed their own customs. They were therefore easily identifiable. They were often persecuted – expelled from some countries, forbidden legal and political rights, even slaughtered in attacks called 'pogroms'.

This persecution was partly the result of the fears and suspicions that Christian inhabitants had of these 'outsiders'. It was also partly because Christians believed that the Jewish people as a whole must carry the blame for the crucifixion of Christ.

'The Final Solution'

The climax of anti-semitism came in Nazi Germany. Hitler believed that the Germans were destined to be the Master Race, but that the Jews were threatening the purity of the German blood.

The campaign against the Jews started with teachers 'picking on' Jewish children in schools and people refusing to buy anything in Jewish shops or to be treated by Jewish doctors. Then Jewish shops and synagogues were attacked. Then laws were passed forbidding intermarriage. Then Jews were arrested and put in concentration camps. Eventually came the 'Final

Anti-semitism

In 1938 Hitler took control of Austria. This photograph was taken in August of that year and shows elderly Jews in Vienna being humiliated: they are being jeered at by Nazis as they are forced to scrub the streets

Solution'; the systematic slaughter of all Jews in German-occupied Europe. Nearly six million perished in what is often called the 'Holocaust'.

Anti-semitism today

Many people in countries other than Germany were anti-semitic. Indeed the most serious pogroms were in Russia; and Jews continue to be discriminated against in Russia today. But when the full horror of the Holocaust was made known at the end of the Second World War, it was generally realized that the Jews had been treated very cruelly for centuries. One of the first actions therefore was the creation of Israel, so that the Jewish people could have a country of their own. However, the Israelis treated the Arab people of Palestine very badly (see p. 73). And so there have been outbursts of anti-semitism again, especially in France. Most frequently it is a symbolic action such as daubing swastikas (the Nazi sign) on synagogues. But sometimes Jewish people have also been killed.

In 1981 eighty graves were badly damaged in a Paris Jewish cemetery by a gang belonging to the New French Nazi Front. Notice their initials in the swastika. The message daubed over the names reads: 'Unworthy of belonging to the new Europe'

Different skin colour

The most common form of racialism today is the dislike of people with dark-coloured skins.

The brownness of a person's complexion is caused by a pigment called 'melanin'. It protects the skin from burning. This is how we get tanned sunbathing. Over the hundreds of thousands of years that man has evolved people born with dark skins have obviously survived better than light-skinned people in the very hot countries.

Skin colour is nothing more nor less than natural adaptation. And yet it is widely felt that coloured people are in some way inferior to white people. It is a surprisingly widespread and subtle belief. It is found, for example, in Brazil and India as well as in more obvious countries like America and South Africa. People with dark brown skins are treated as inferior to people with light brown skins. How do you think this has happened?

Prejudice against Blacks

Early European contacts

The great majority of people with dark brown skins are of the negroid race. To distinguish them from light brown people they are now usually called Blacks. These people are of African origin.

Now, during the past 200 years or so when Europeans have had a lot of dealings with Africa, African people have been living in comparatively primitive life-styles. The Europeans knew that, in contrast, the Chinese, Indians and Arabs had civilizations stretching back many centuries. However, they knew nothing about African history when great kingdoms flourished, particularly in West Africa, and which often had standards of living and a culture higher than many European countries. However Europeans believed that the African people had 'just come out of the jungle'. At the end of the nineteenth century European countries swiftly took control of the whole of the African continent.

Slavery

This belief in the inferiority of negroid people seemed to be confirmed by the slave trade. Black people were captured in Africa, transported in ships across the Atlantic Ocean and sold to plantation-owners as slaves. By the early nineteenth century millions of black slaves were working on cotton, sugar and fruit plantations in Brazil, on the islands of the West Indies and in the United States.

Present-day problems

The negroid people of the world have therefore had huge disadvantages to overcome. And although within a fairly short time many have become very distinguished, the old prejudices linger on.

Black people more than any others have suffered from the white man's double catch. Black people have not been allowed the same educational and job opportunities as white people; therefore fewer black people are successful in the professions and in business; therefore the white people argue that this proves the inferiority of the Blacks.

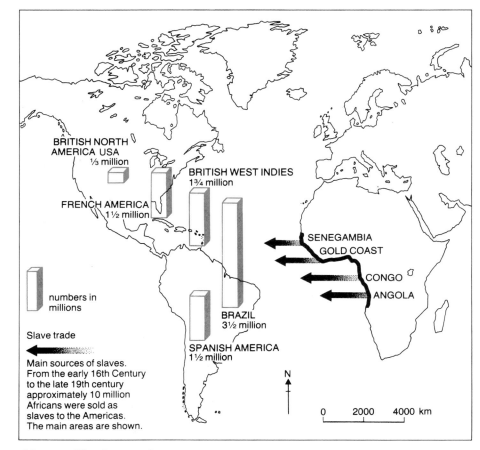

Map 2   The slave trade

Freeing the American slaves

Civil war

No country has suffered more bitterly from the effects of slavery than the United States of America. In the middle of the last century there were over three million slaves in the USA, about 14% of the population. The vast majority of these were in the southern states, so that in some areas there were as many black slaves as white people. In the 1860s a terrible civil war was fought between the northern and southern states. One of the quarrels concerned the abolition of slavery which was ordered by the President, Abraham Lincoln. The north won and the slaves were freed.

Continuing disadvantages

Even so, for another 100 years negroes remained 'second-class citizens'. They were forced to take hard, low-paid jobs – even those who drifted to the big northern cities in search of a better life. Schools and housing were poor.

In the southern states:

1 Negroes were prevented from using the same buses or restaurants as white people;

2 they were prevented from voting;

3 white gangs called the Ku Klux Klan even murdered black people and were not brought to trial (see p. 75).

The KKK was formed in the southern states of the USA to persecute negroes freed from slavery during the Civil War (note the Confederate flag). It has been revived most recently to fight the Civil Rights Movement. This photograph was taken in Little Rock, Arkansas in 1979

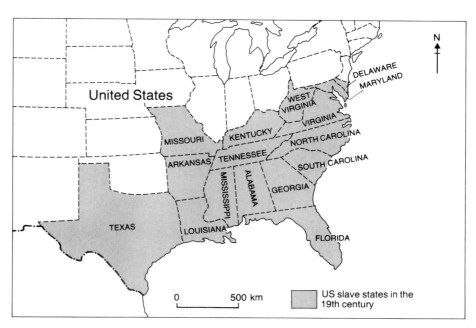

Map 3   *Slave states in the USA in the 19th century*

USA

Some improvements

In the 1950s and 1960s especially, four different ways were used to improve the lot of the American Blacks:

Government

The government and the courts of law made the southern states treat the Blacks as equals with the Whites, particularly in education and voting rights. Later there were schemes of 'positive discrimination'. These were arrangements for giving areas with black people privileged treatment, such as extra money for new buildings.

Riots

Black people in the slums of some northern cities demonstrated violently against their conditions. Great damage was done in parts of Los Angeles, Detroit and Newark.

Peaceful demonstrations

Huge civil rights demonstrations were organized, most successfully by the Revd. Martin Luther King (see p. 75). People paraded to demand equal treatment with Whites.

Black Power

However, some black people have felt that they will never be treated equally while they try to compete with white people who have all the advantages. Some have even believed that they should work for a separate black country in part of the USA. Many have rejected Christianity as the white man's religion and have become Muslims (see p. 64). The most famous is the boxer, Cassius Clay, who took the new Muslim name of Mohammed Ali.

Before 4 am, on 1 November 1976 over 5000 people (mainly unemployed Blacks), started queuing outside the Cadillac car works in Detroit, though no work was available

Mohammed Ali, after saying he wished to become an Islamic evangelist, 1981

However, despite all the improvements, the black people of the USA still suffer from poor conditions. A much larger proportion of Blacks than Whites are unemployed or live in poverty-stricken conditions. Since the mid-1970s unemployment has increased enormously so that in many cities it is almost impossible for a young black to find a job at all.

6.6 Britain

British 'immigrants'

Where have they come from?

Britain has a tradition of receiving immigrants from overseas, who come either because of job opportunities or as refugees. Many Irish, Jews, Chinese and Poles, for example, have settled in Britain over the past century or so.

How have coloured people come to be in Britain? For about half a century from the 1890s Britain had the largest empire the world has ever known. Then, very quickly from the late 1940s, to the late 1960s, Britain gave independence to her former colonies. However, until quite recently it was never made very clear whether or not the people of these former colonies were British citizens and therefore had the right to live and settle in Britain.

In fact, many such people did immigrate into Britain particularly in the 1960s (see fig. 1, p. 87).

Why have they come?

As the countries of Europe, including Britain, recovered from the Second World War, it was discovered that there were not enough workers for some of the necessary jobs. And so, for example, Germany recruited workers from Turkey; France, from Algeria. In Britain the hospitals and London Transport in particular were very grateful for the people from the West Indies and India who replied to advertisements for jobs in Britain.

Where have they settled?

These 'immigrants' tended to congregate where there was work and cheap housing. So people of the same race tended to live close to each other. Coloured people therefore became concentrated in a small number of cities: in London, Leicester, Birmingham, Liverpool, Manchester, and Bradford in particular.

Some families have been in Britain for so long now that it is misleading to call them 'immigrants'. As the years go by an increasing proportion of multi-racial people have been born in Britain and know no other country. There are now about 1.75 million coloured people in Britain, that is, about 3% of the whole population.

Prejudice and discrimination

Luckily there have not been race riots in Britain as serious as those in the USA. However, race relations have not been all that easy. Tense relations with the local police forces, for example, sparked off severe rioting in several city areas in recent years, notably in Bristol, Brixton (London), and Toxteth (Liverpool).

Brixton, South London, 13 April 1981: after two nights of rioting, arson and looting, hundreds of rioters and policemen were injured. An inquiry into the disturbances was held afterwards by the judge, Lord Scarman. Although the West Indian rioters committed criminal acts, the police were criticized for being racially prejudiced and using provocative methods

Britain

Two examples

Here are two quotations which show the kind of problems that have developed in Britain:

❝ Most innocent West Indians came to this country because they were promised a new and better life. They came. They worked for long hours every day to earn their bread, help build up the country and now when they're just ready to reap the benefits Mr Powell wants them thrown out.

I think racial hatred is stemmed from the early days when slavery was abolished. I don't think the majority of the whites could bring themselves to accept the Black Man as an equal. All his life the Black Man has been intimidated and looked down upon . . . All his life he has had to settle for second best. And I think now that today's West Indians are realizing that fact and want to do something about it.

That's why many black people today hate the white man generally. Although its a narrow minded view of life it just simply represents their feelings. ❞
(R. Jeffcoate, *Positive Image*, 1979)

George Tonkin, a Welshman whose skin turned brown through a kidney disease:

❝ Suddenly Britain and even my home town had become places where if I walked on the streets I faced insults. Where if I went into a pub, I risked being snubbed. Where if I went for a job there were automatically no vacancies. I became one of those men who some people love to hate. I had become a coloured man. Since the change of colour I can feel a change in my personality. I have become more wary and withdrawn. I have to be on guard all the time. Because of my colour I go as little as possible to London. If I do I go by car. I've read about this Paki-bashing. I hate going on tubes and buses just in case there's a skinhead ready to put the boot in. I know my fears are probably not justified. But I now realize that these are the same fears thousands of coloured people living in Britain have every day. ❞

The extract is from Mr Tonkin's story in *The News of the World*. Tonkin died in December 1970 following a kidney-transplant operation which he hoped would turn him white again. He was 31.

Enoch Powell

Most politicians have been very careful to persuade people of different races to be tolerant towards each other. There has been one important exception: Mr Enoch Powell.

He has foretold serious racial conflict. In a speech attacking the government for allowing relatives of immigrants already in Britain to join them, he said:

❝ We must be mad, literally mad as a nation to be permitting the annual inflow of 50 000 dependants . . . it is like watching a nation busily engaged in heaping up its own funeral pyre. ❞

He has suggested that multi-racial groups should be sent back to their country of origin.

Mr Enoch Powell, MP

The National Front (NF)

Enoch Powell is worried by what he foresees. But more dangerous is the National Front. This is a political party, although it has no members in parliament. Its members are willing to stir up racial hatred by propaganda and demonstrations in areas inhabited by multi-racial groups.

Members of the National Front (youth section) demonstrating for a 'white' Britain

Britain

What has the Government done?

The Government has passed a number of laws over the years to try to keep race relations as happy as possible. These laws have been of two main kinds: to limit the number of immigrants allowed to enter Britain and to prevent discrimination against those already settled. Most of these laws were passed in the 1960s when there were particularly large numbers of multi-racial groups entering Britain (see fig. 1). The most recent laws are:

The Race Relations Act, 1976

This act set up the Commission for Racial Equality to improve understanding between white and coloured people and to stamp out discrimination.

British Nationality Act, 1981

This act tried to define who exactly are British citizens and who therefore has a right to live in Britain. It is very complicated and some experts think that it is unfair on some coloured people.

The future?

White and coloured people live in Britain in relative harmony. Do you think that this is likely to last? There are conflicting clues.

Each summer there is a great street carnival organized by coloured people in Notting Hill in London. In its early years there was violence. But in recent years the event has been a very happy one.

On the other hand, coloured and especially black people have been particularly seriously affected by the rise in unemployment in recent times. Some black youths, perhaps because of this, have drifted into crime. In 1981 a number of black people were involved in street riots which were especially serious in the Toxteth district of Liverpool and the Brixton district of London. What was the cause: unemployment, crime or police harassment? Probably a mixture of all.

Furthermore, by the beginning of 1985 there was evidence of a serious increase in racialist attacks – especially against Asians in East London. Bangladeshi families have been abused and harassed; bricks have been thrown through windows; lighted rags, and excrement have been pushed through letter-boxes; shops vandalized; people beaten, knifed and kicked.

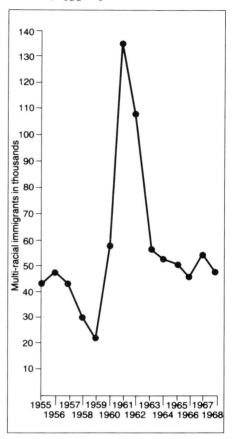

Fig 1   Multi-racial immigration into Britain, 1955–1968

People in West London whose families came from the West Indies strive to retain their Caribbean culture especially through the annual Notting Hill Carnival

The peoples of South Africa

The most difficult and dangerous problems of race relations are in South Africa. This is a large and rich country with a very mixed population (see fig 2):

1 By far the largest numbers are the black negroid people.

2 The next largest group are the Whites. Some of these are descendants of Dutch people who started to settle in the country 300 years ago. These are called 'Afrikaners'. Other white people are descendants of British people who started to settle there just over 150 years ago.

3 Some people are 'coloured'. This word has a very special meaning in South Africa: it is used to describe people of mixed race.

4 There are also a small number of people of Indian and Chinese origin.

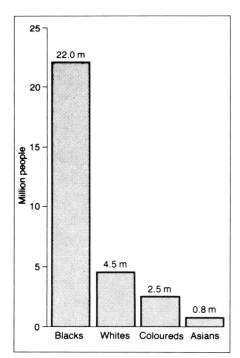

Fig 2 The racial composition of South Africa

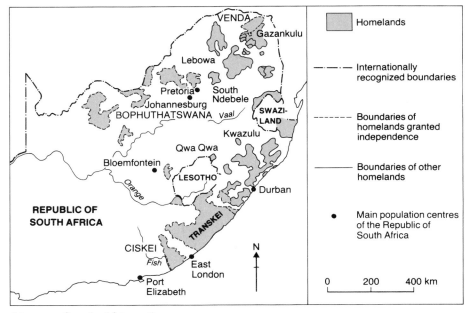

Map 4 South African Bantustans

What is 'apartheid'?

Ever since white people settled in the country they have been in charge. But since the late 1940s a very particular set of arrangements have been introduced to try to keep the Whites and Blacks separated. This system is called 'apartheid' – literally 'apart-ness' in Afrikaans. It takes two forms.

'Grand apartheid'

The eventual aim is, theoretically, for the Blacks to be confined to certain parts of South Africa while the Whites have the rest. Just over 13% of the country has been allotted to the Blacks. These lands are called 'Bantustans'. Gradually the government is giving them so-called independence, though in fact the Bantustans have no real chance of being properly independent.

'Petty apartheid'

A great number of laws have been passed to try to keep black and white people separate while the black people are still living and working in 'white' South Africa. At their most harsh these laws have prevented Blacks and Whites from marrying; using the same buses, park seats or restaurants; playing in the same sports teams, for example. In 1978 Mr P W Botha became Prime Minister and in 1984, President. He has introduced a few reforms. But the improvements for the black people have been very small.

Notice restricting the use of a beach

Apartheid

Arguments for and against

Arguments for

The supporters of the apartheid system argue that it is best for everyone. White people have developed the land into the richest country in Africa and therefore they should be allowed to enjoy the results. Furthermore, the black people also benefit because they enjoy, on average, a higher standard of living than black people in any other African country. Afrikaners also believe that black and white people want to live different lives and should therefore be allowed to do so separately.

Arguments against

However, most other countries in the world are quite sure that the system is cruelly unjust. As a result, the United Nations has condemned apartheid and many countries will not allow their cricketers and rugby players to play against the racially segregated South African teams. Also many people believe that civil war will one day break out if the government, which is controlled by the Afrikaners, does not treat the Blacks more justly.

What, then, are the objections to apartheid?

1 It is obviously unfair that the black majority should be allowed only a tiny fraction of the total land of the country as Bantustans (73% of the population has been allocated 13.73% of the land).

2 Complete separation is, in fact, quite impossible. The cities, factories and mines of 'white' South Africa could not continue to run without a great number of black workers.

3 The Blacks are treated as inferior people. All the best jobs are reserved for Whites.

These demonstrators are saying that if the British rugby team toured South Africa, it would be tantamount to kicking the Blacks in the face

Nelson Mandela, a leader of the African National Congress, was arrested, 1962, and placed in an island prison for defying the South African Government

Apartheid

4 Any opposition or demonstrations against apartheid, however mild and peaceful, are brutally crushed by the police. Some of the most famous black leaders have been arrested and have been in prison for many years. The most important is Nelson Mandela, who has been in prison since 1962. Peaceful demonstrations of black people at the towns of Sharpeville in 1960 and Soweto in 1976 have been dispersed by the police shooting and killing many of the crowd.

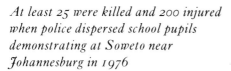

At least 25 were killed and 200 injured when police dispersed school pupils demonstrating at Soweto near Johannesburg in 1976

6.8 Conclusion

Most of the obvious examples of unfairness and discrimination between different races happen *inside* rather than between various countries. And when the coloured people become particularly angry, they demonstrate and riot.

However, the unfairness of the white people being rich and the coloured people being poor is world-wide. Most of the rich countries of the world are where white people live; and most of the poor countries of the world are where the coloured people live. Apart from the Arab countries which have become rich through oil, it is the black, brown and yellow races of the world who are poor.

What is more, the differences in wealth between 'white' countries and 'coloured' countries are becoming greater. The physical differences of race are being deepened by the economic differences of wealth. And the increasing feeling of injustice among the coloured races could lead to most dreadful violent conflicts.

Black people in particular have made a number of attempts to reassert their dignity. During the present century people of negroid race have declared their pride in their race, wherever they might be living – in the USA, the West Indies, or Africa for example. And they have reminded themselves and the rest of the world that they have a distinctive culture. Slogans have been coined like 'Black is beautiful' (in the USA) and 'négritude' (in French-speaking West Africa).

Questions

1 a Why is it difficult to classify races?
  b What is the difference between 'prejudice' and 'discrimination'?
  c What have been the causes of anti-semitism?
  d Why has there been so much prejudice against black people?
  e How have the conditions of black people in the USA improved in recent times?
  f Why are there coloured people living in Britain today?
  g What is apartheid?
  h Why do you think racial prejudice and discrimination are bad?

2 Write an essay or hold a class discussion on whether ethnic minorities should live in separate groups or be assimilated into the English community.

3 Read the following passages and answer the questions on each.

❛ History has shown with terrible clarity that each time Aryan blood has become mixed with inferior peoples the result has been the end of the culture-sustaining race. . . .

The result of every racial crossing, to put it briefly, is always as follows:
(a) sinking of the standard of the higher race;
(b) physical and mental deterioration and the beginning of a slow but certain and progressive chronic ill-health. . . .

All that we admire on this earth – science, art, technical skill and invention – is the creative product of only a small number of nations, and originally, perhaps, of one single race. All this culture depends on them for its very existence. If these nations are ruined, they carry with them all the beauty of this earth into the grave. . . .

Who wants to live also must fight, and he who does not want to fight in this world does not deserve to live. . . .

If mankind were to be divided into three categories, into founders, maintainers, and destroyers of culture, the Aryan stock alone would represent the first category of founders. From them come the fundamentals of all human creative effort. . . . ❜

Adolf Hitler, *Mein Kampf* (1925)

  a What does the word 'Aryan' mean? Why did Hitler think that the Aryans were so important?
  b What arguments does Hitler use here in favour of racial purity? Is there any truth in his arguments?
  c What is the meaning of the word 'culture'?
  d Why does Hitler believe that fighting is necessary?

❛ In government we will not be satisfied with anything less than direct individual adult suffrage and the right to stand for and be elected to all organs of government.

In economic matters we will be satisfied with nothing less than equality of opportunity in every sphere, and the enjoyment by all of those heritages which form the resources of the country which up to now have been appropriated on a racial 'Whites only' basis.

In culture we will be satisfied with nothing less than the opening of all doors of learning in non-segregatory institutions on the sole criterion of ability.

In the social sphere we will be satisfied with nothing less than the abolition of all racial bars.

We do not demand these things for people of African descent alone. We demand them for all South Africans, white and black. ❜

Chief Albert Luthuli, speech on acceptance of the Nobel Peace Prize for 1960

  a What does the phrase 'adult suffrage' mean?
  b What does the phrase 'Whites only' mean?
  c Compare the passages from Hitler and Luthuli. Compare the arguments for treating people of different races according to the principles of:
  (i) the best and the strongest, and (ii) equality.

❛ [In] that popular television series, *Till Death us do Part*, the idea was supposed to be that viewers would ridicule Alf Garnett and identify with the young couple, his modern daughter and son-in-law. But instead, Alf Garnett became a folk-hero. The programme had exceedingly bad effects; words like 'coon' freely used by Alf, were repeated by white men to black work-mates, the racist clichés that sprinkled his conversation passed into the vocabulary not only of adults but of child viewers, and thousands of black people were angered and distressed by this popularization and repetition of the crudest kind of race jokes. However, the BBC seemed to think that critics were being very naïve and unsophisticated in not understanding that the programme was meant to be making fun of racism and seemed quite uninterested in the evidence of those who should, after all, know best what effect it was having – the people at the receiving end of the racist jeering and hostility. ❜

Ann Dummett, *A Portrait of English Racism* (1973)

  a Have you seen any films or read any comics which give false views of coloured people?
  b Why is the word 'coon' offensive?
  c What effect do you think that television generally has on race relations?

7 Poverty in the Third World

Street scenes: Lagos, Nigeria, and Hull, England. Britain's Gross National Product per head (per capita GNP, an indication of average wealth) is about eight times that of Nigeria.

7.1 Tests of poverty

Contrasts

What we take for granted

Almost everyone in Britain (and in other rich countries like the USA, West Germany and Australia) enjoys a good standard of living. People have enough food to eat, clothes to keep them warm, and somewhere to live. Most people have radios and televisions. A lot of people even have refrigerators and cars. Many of us take these living conditions for granted.

It is difficult to imagine living in constant hunger, with no proper

sanitation or running water, and with the likelihood of dying quite young from a crippling disease. But that is what *real* poverty means. And it is the lot of hundreds of millions of people in the world today.

The Third World

The poorer countries of the world are often called the 'Third World'. The rich countries of the western world, like America and Western Europe, are the 'First World'. Communist countries like Russia and Eastern Europe are the 'Second World'. The poorer countries are

also sometimes called 'under-developed' or 'Less Developed Countries' (LDCs for short) (see map 6, p. 98).

This means that most of the people of these countries are living in conditions less affected by industry and technology than the 'First' and 'Second' Worlds. As a result the average standard of living is quite low. Most of the rich countries are in the northern half of the planet; most of the poor countries are in the southern half, as you can see from map 1.

Tests of poverty

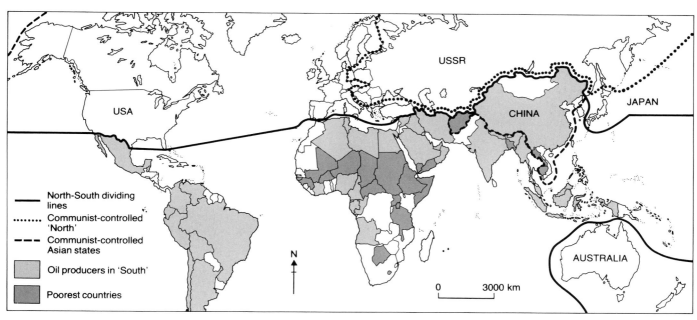

Map 1   The 'North-South' division of the world

Key:
- North-South dividing lines
- Communist-controlled 'North'
- Communist-controlled Asian states
- Oil producers in 'South'
- Poorest countries

0   3000 km

There are wealthy people even in a country like India where there is much poverty (Britain's per capita GNP is about 30 times that of India). This photograph was taken in Calcutta

Differences inside countries

When we talk about 'poor' countries we are referring to the *average* income or wealth of the people. But in some of these poor countries there are a number of people who are very rich indeed. For example, in India there are the descendants of the former princes and maharajahs; in oil-rich countries in the Middle East, like Saudi Arabia, there are the privileged sheikhs. When there are such sharp contrasts it is much more difficult to bear the poverty if you are one of the majority who are poor.

Measuring a country's wealth or poverty

How do we decide whether a person is rich or not? We can ask various questions about them to find out. For example, we could ask what he or she owns (the size of their house for example) or how much the person earns in wages or salary a year.

There are similar questions, or tests, we can use for countries to find out if they are rich or poor. It is possible to compare the levels of poverty in different countries by comparing certain figures, or 'statistics', that are available:

1 *Average* wealth can be measured in two ways; by 'per capita GDP' or by 'per capita GNP'. A country produces wealth by agriculture, mining, industry and trade. GDP (Gross Domestic Product) is the total of a country's *internal* (or domestic) wealth (see fig. 1, p. 98); GNP (Gross National Product) is the total of GDP plus the country's *national* wealth (i.e. it includes payments made and received for 'services', like banking and insurance). If you divide the GNP by the population of the country you can discover the average wealth produced by each individual ('per capita' as it is called). This is the equation:

$$\frac{GNP}{population} = \text{per capita GNP}$$

Per capita GNP gives a useful clue as to the likely average wage. The poorest countries in the world have a per capita GNP of about \$150 (see map 4, p. 97).

93

Tests of poverty

2 *Hunger* can be measured by average calorie intake (map 2, p. 96).

3 *Disease and death* can be measured by infant mortality rates and by the average age of death (see map 3, p. 96).

4 *Education* can be measured by literacy rates (see map 5, p. 97).

Malnutrition and death rates

Lack of food

Hundreds of millions of people do not have enough to eat. The poorest of these live constantly on the edge of starvation (see map 2, p. 96). Many, especially children, suffer from 'malnutrition' – that is, their diet is not properly balanced for good health. Poor people often cannot afford sufficient protein. So many people are hungry either because they live in parts of the world with infertile soil, or because they are too poor to be able to buy food.

For many of these poor people hunger is a vicious circle. Because they are under-nourished or mal-nourished they are too weak to work properly; because they do not work properly they cannot produce enough food for themselves or earn enough wages.

Disease

Undernourishment and malnutrition lower the body's resistance to disease. And again people suffering from serious illnesses cannot work properly. Many millions of poor people, especially in Africa, suffer from diseases like malaria, sleeping sickness, river-blindness. Bilharzia (an illness caused by parasitic worms attacking the blood and bladder) alone affects about 200 million people. And it is estimated that 20 000 children die of diarrhoea *each day*.

Average weekly food intake for someone living in the first World (left) and in the Third World (right). An individual's basic food needs are measured in calories: 1600 per day is a critical minimum; 2400 is the average need. In the UK the average daily calorie intake per person is 3316. In Ethiopia it is 1729. Of course this does not show the many millions below the average

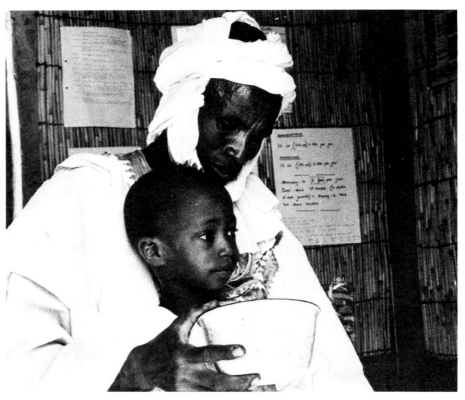

This child in Burkina Faso (West Africa) is being given a sugar and salt solution to counteract the dehydration which resulted from his diarrhoea

94

Tests of poverty

Death rates

In rich countries like Britain most people can expect to live until the age of about 70. In poor countries the *average* age of death is about 40 or 50 (see map 3, p. 96). The two main reasons for this wide difference are hunger and disease:

1 In poor countries many babies die because they are not properly fed and therefore easily catch diseases;

2 and some of the diseases listed gradually kill the adults who suffer from them.

Living conditions

The living conditions of many people are extremely poor. This is particularly noticeable in the large cities of the Third World, such as Calcutta in India; Mexico City; Manila in the Philippines. In these great sprawling cities live millions of people with barely adequate shelter. 'Shanty towns' have sprung up on the edge of many such cities where the desperately poor put up 'houses' of whatever materials come to hand – old oil drums, strips of corrugated iron, even cardboard. There is often no clean water supply, so disease spreads very quickly.

Literacy

Many people in the Third World can neither read nor write. The number of illiterate people in poor conditions is so high for the following reasons:

1 Money is not available to build schools or pay teachers.

2 Children do not go to school because they are needed by their families for work.

A lot of poor peasants move from the countryside to the cities in search of work. But most of them are illiterate. It is very difficult to teach

The 'barriadas' (slums) of Lima, Peru, have no lighting, water or sanitation

people skills for jobs if they cannot read. And jobs in towns, particularly in industry, often require the ability to read, even if only simple notices.

What can be done? The problem of illiteracy, like the problem of hunger, is a vicious circle. Countries with low standards of education cannot easily increase their wealth. But to improve their standards of

education they must build schools and pay teachers. And that needs money. UNESCO (see p. 44) has tried to break this vicious circle by sending volunteer teachers to countries most in need of help. Great progress has been made in some countries. But there are still about 800 million people in the world who are totally illiterate (see map 5, p. 97).

An adult literacy class in Mexico which has been organized by UNESCO

Tests of poverty

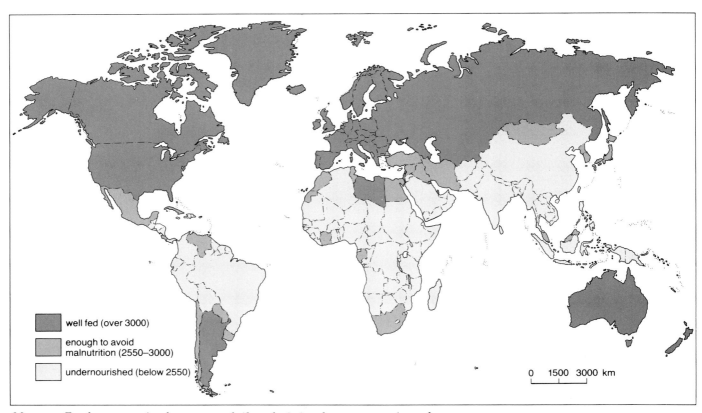

Map 2   Food consumption by average daily calorie intake per person in each country

well fed (over 3000)

enough to avoid
malnutrition (2550–3000)

undernourished (below 2550)

0   1500   3000 km

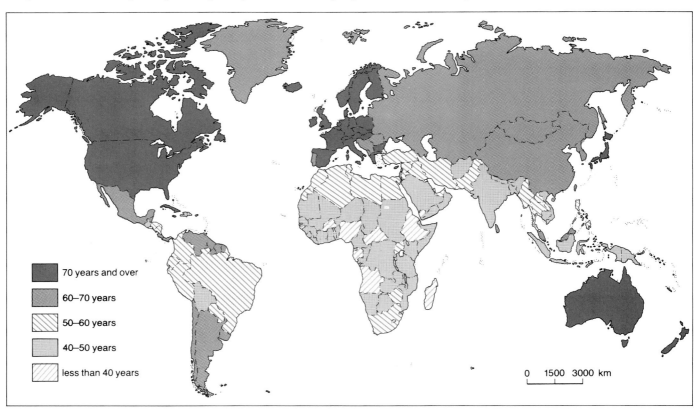

Map 3   Average life expectancy at birth

70 years and over

60–70 years

50–60 years

40–50 years

less than 40 years

0   1500   3000 km

Tests of poverty

Map 4   Per capita GNP in 1981, in US dollars

above $7000

$3000–$7000

$1500–$3000

$750–$1500

$300–$750

below $300

data not available

0   1500   3000 km

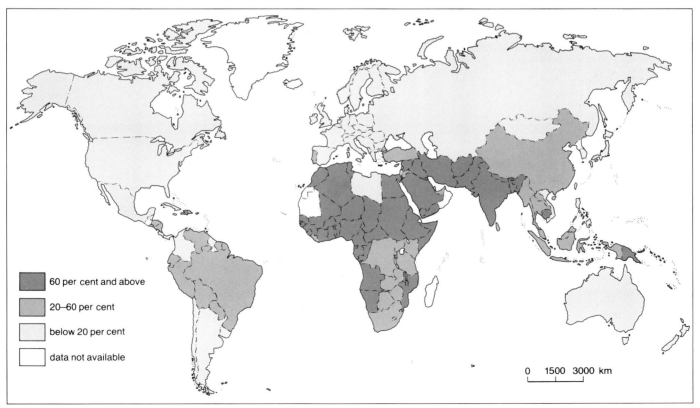

Map 5   Illiterates as a proportion of the population, 15 years and over

60 per cent and above

20–60 per cent

below 20 per cent

data not available

0   1500   3000 km

97

7.2 Range of poverty

The poorest countries

Some countries are so poor that the United Nations has made a list of those that need very special help – the Least Developed Countries (LLDCs). Map 6, below, shows where these LLDCs are. Compare maps 2–5 with what *The Brandt Report* of 1980 has to say, see pp. 106–107.)

‘ Most of the Least Developed Countries . . . are found contiguously (*that is, next to each other*) in two areas which we call the 'poverty belts'* . . .

(*Each country*) has a slim margin between subsistence and disaster. . . . This condition has worsened in the 1970s. ’

(* *You can see the 'poverty belts' shown on map 6, below.*)
About 300 million people live in these conditions of direst poverty.

	GDP '82 $	% illiterate	Life expectancy
Bangladesh	121	74	40–50
Benin	221	72	40–50
Botswana	830	59	40–50
Ethiopia	97	87	c. 40
Haiti	228	79	40–50
Laos	91	56	50–60
Tanzania	254	26	40–50
N Yemen	215	73	c. 40
UK	7192	c. 10	70+

Fig. 1   The UK and eight of the LLDCs

In 1984 the effects of really desparate poverty was most vividly demonstrated by distressing BBC film showing death by starvation of hundreds of thousands of Ethiopian people. Their plight had been caused by a combination of bad agricultural methods, drought and civil war.

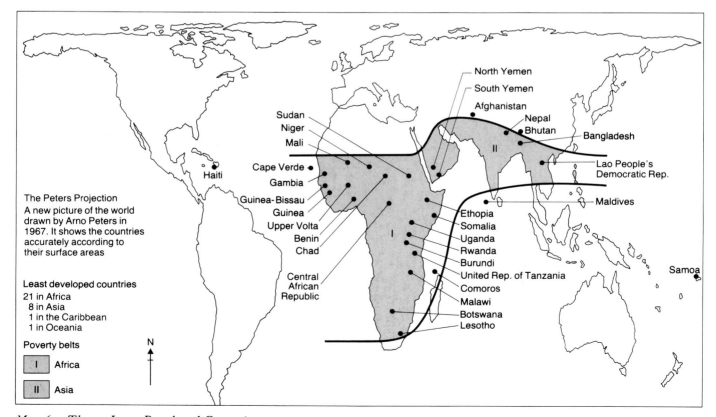

The Peters Projection
A new picture of the world drawn by Arno Peters in 1967. It shows the countries accurately according to their surface areas

Least developed countries
21 in Africa
8 in Asia
1 in the Caribbean
1 in Oceania

Poverty belts
I   Africa
II   Asia

Map 6   The 31 Least Developed Countries

7.3 Reasons for poverty

Campa Indians living in a tropical rain forest in Peru, South America

The dramatic and painful effects of drought in Africa

When we look at the conditions in poor countries it is difficult sometimes to tell what is the *cause* and what is the *effect* of poverty. For example, many people are ill because they cannot afford proper medical attention; but, then, because they are ill, they cannot work properly to produce wealth. That is why the phrase 'vicious circle' has been used (pp. 94 and 95).

In the previous sections we looked at some of the obvious indications of poverty and the kind of statistics that can be used to measure the degree of poverty in a country. In this section we will look at some of the deeper reasons for some countries being so much poorer than others.

Climate and environment

Heat

It is not a coincidence that the poorest countries are also the hottest. When temperatures during the day are about 40°C it is impossible to do a lot of heavy, physical work. So the general pace of work in such countries has to be quite slow.

A hot damp climate easily breeds disease. Insects, such as the malaria-carrying mosquito, breed in these conditions. The great rain forests and river basins such as the Amazon in South America, the Congo in Central Africa, and the Mekong in South-East Asia are such areas.

If, on the other hand, a country has a hot, dry climate, agriculture suffers from lack of irrigation. The area of desert in the world is expanding at a serious rate, especially in the strip of land across Africa to the south of the Sahara Desert known as the Sahel. Desert is made not just by the effects of the sun, but by man's bad management of the soil (see pp. 101 and 137).

Reasons for poverty

Natural disasters

Farmers are able to plan regular planting and harvesting only if they can be assured of regular climatic conditions. Some countries, however, suffer very serious droughts and/or flooding. These natural disasters are especially serious in Asiatic countries like China, India, and Bangladesh. But it is not only that plants are shrivelled by drought or swept away by floods. Drought also reduces the supply of clean water necessary for drinking and sanitation: floods also destroy roads and houses.

Lack of natural wealth and industry

The importance of mineral wealth

If a country's wealth depends almost entirely on agriculture, it is impossible for its standard of living to rise very high. Some countries which have been poor have been able to become richer by selling precious minerals from their land. The most obvious examples are countries in the Middle East which have been able to earn huge sums of money from oil.

The problem of the countries which remain especially poor, like those in West Africa, is that their lands do not contain any such natural wealth. In other countries, like those in central Africa, natural wealth does exist, but they do not have enough money to pay for prospectors and equipment to mine it.

The importance of industry

The wealth of most of the rich countries of the world comes largely from industry. Factories are able to produce clothes, furniture, and agricultural machines, for example, to raise the standard of living of the people in industrialized countries. And manufactured goods can also be sold abroad; so the money earned by this trade can be used for buying even more goods for the people.

Some countries that have been poor, like South Korea and Taiwan for example, have raised their standard of living considerably in recent years by expanding their industries. They have been able to do this, even though they have few natural resources, by making goods which other countries are willing to buy. How many manufactured goods do you have in your home from these Asian countries? The really poor countries of the world are those with very little industry.

Over-population

What is happening?

You have only to look at the cartoon opposite to see how dramatically the population of the world has increased in recent years. What is more, the numbers are still increasing at an alarming rate. Over one million people are added to the population of the world every five days. It is estimated that by the year 2000 the world will contain about 6 000 000 000 people. The single most important reason for the increase is the improvement in health conditions so that, on average, people are living much longer than they used to. However, by the mid-1980s the speed of population increase seemed to be slowing down.

Jaunpur, eastern India, in 1980 when about 500 people died in floods

Reasons for poverty

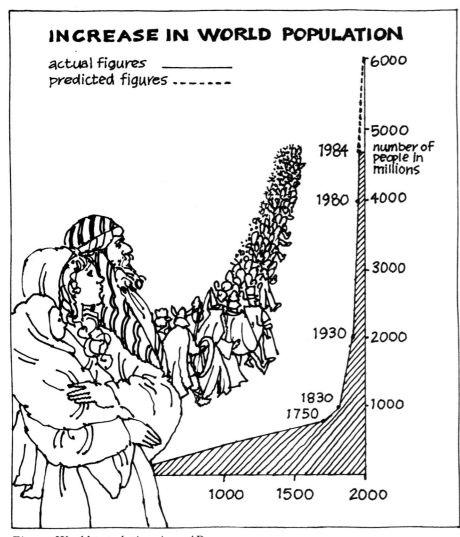

INCREASE IN WORLD POPULATION

actual figures —————
predicted figures - - - - - -

number of people in millions

6000
5000
4000
3000
2000
1000

1984
1980
1930
1830
1750

1000   1500   2000

Fig 2   World population since AD

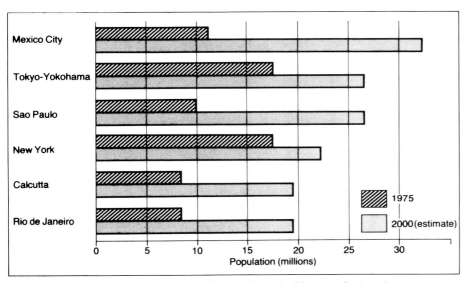

Mexico City
Tokyo-Yokohama
Sao Paulo
New York
Calcutta
Rio de Janeiro

0   5   10   15   20   25   30
Population (millions)

1975
2000 (estimate)

Fig 3   Some of the largest cities of the world ranked by population size

What are the effects?

The increase in the world's population has happened so suddenly that we speak of a population 'explosion'. It is one of the most serious problems facing the world – for the following reasons:

1 *Pressure on land.*   As more and more people try to live off the land, it becomes exhausted. Land that is over-farmed without being replenished with fertilizer becomes desert (pp. 99 and 137). As forests are cleared – to make room for more agricultural land and to use the wood for fuel – that land too becomes desert (see pp. 136–137).

2 *Pressure on food supplies.*   The more people there are in the world, the more mouths there are to feed. Food production has, in fact, increased considerably in recent years (see pp. 103, 138–139). But, even so, it has not been able to keep pace. As a result, as we have seen on pp. 94 and 96, huge numbers of people are suffering from undernourishment and malnutrition.

3 *Pressure on cities.*   As the populations of some of the biggest cities increase, so housing sprawls out over a very large area. A new word has been invented to describe such a vast place. It is 'megalopolis' and means 'huge city'. In some of the biggest cities in the poorer countries, it has become impossible to provide essential services like housing, water, sewerage and lighting.

4 *Unemployment.*   As more and more children grow up an increasing number of people, especially in the cities and towns, are looking for work. Millions fail to find regular employment. Without wages they remain poor.

Reasons for poverty

Poverty is made worse by huge families like this one in Paraguay

Particular problems of the Third World

1 *Scale of the problem.* It is estimated that two billion extra people will be added to the population of the world during the 1980s and 1990s. About 1.8 billion of these will be in the Third World. Map 7 shows the different rates of population increase. Percentages here can be deceptive. The population of a country doubles in about 30 years if the annual increase is a little over two per cent!

2 *Lack of contraception.* Many people in poor countries do not use any methods of contraception. There are several reasons for this:

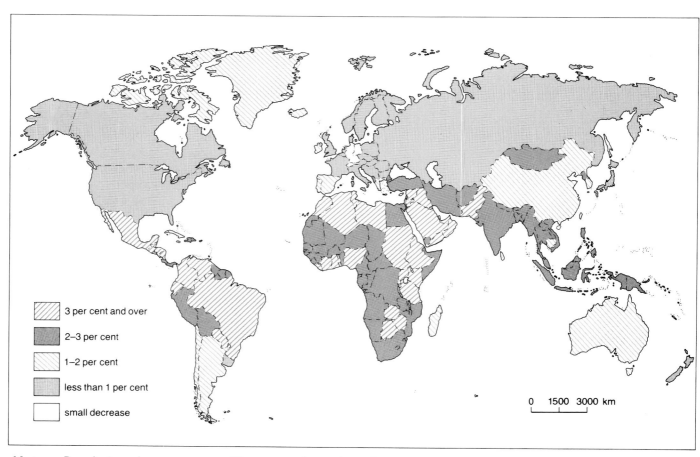

3 per cent and over

2–3 per cent

1–2 per cent

less than 1 per cent

small decrease

0   1500   3000 km

Map 7   Population: the average rate of increase each year in each country

Reasons for poverty

a) The Roman Catholic church forbids contraception. It regards it as a sin. The majority of the people in Central and South America are devout Roman Catholics.
b) Poor people cannot afford to buy contraceptives. Nor are there many clinics to help people in these countries.
c) People want to have a larger number of children.

3 *The desire for large families.* Many adults in poor countries feel that they need to have many children. This is partly because a high proportion of babies die and partly because they need young people to help with work, for example in producing food.

Political troubles

Many Third World countries have suffered serious political problems. As a result their governments have not concentrated on tackling the problems of poverty. Until recently many of these countries were colonies. They have found it difficult to organize settled governments. Quarrels have led to bloodshed, and in some cases to civil war (see p. 4).

Unfair trading patterns

Poor countries are often unable to obtain fair or assured prices for the products they export. These problems are discussed in chapter 8.

7.4 How can conditions be improved

Increase in production

Food

Food production and food supplies can be increased in a number of different ways (see also pp. 138–139):

1 *Machinery.* Using tractors, and seed-drills for example.

2 *Artificial fertilizer.* This is used to supplement the insufficient amounts of animal manure.

3 *Water control.* Irrigation schemes for regular supplies of water and protection against flooding.

4 *Improved crops.* The 'Green Revolution'. Scientists have produced variants of some crops which grow more abundantly or which can be harvested several times a year.

5 *Pesticides.* Huge quantities of food are destroyed each year by insects attacking plants, and animals (like rats and mice) eating food in stores. Increased use of pesticides can reduce this loss.

6 *Transport.* In some countries people are hungry not because the country is short of food but because it is not possible to transport stocks from one part of the country to another. Improved roads and railways help to cope with this problem.

7 *Training.* Teaching people to farm most efficiently according to the land that they have.

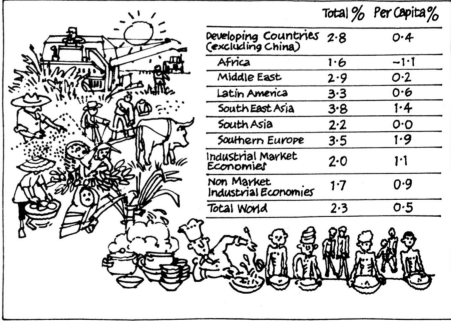

AVERAGE ANNUAL GROWTH IN FOOD OUTPUT

	Total %	Per Capita %
Developing Countries (excluding China)	2·8	0·4
Africa	1·6	–1·1
Middle East	2·9	0·2
Latin America	3·3	0·6
South East Asia	3·8	1·4
South Asia	2·2	0·0
Southern Europe	3·5	1·9
Industrial Market Economies	2·0	1·1
Non Market Industrial Economies	1·7	0·9
Total World	2·3	0·5

Increases made in food output are eroded by population growth, 1970–1980. Can you name the parts of the world which: a) produced less food in comparison with its population; b) increased its food production most; c) had the greatest population increase?

How can conditions be improved?

Many Third World cities have expanded and been modernized very quickly. This scene is in downtown Rio de Janeiro, Brazil

Industry and mining

If Third World countries can produce oil, mine metal-ores and manufacture industrial goods themselves, they can increase their wealth. Two sets of countries have managed to increase their wealth in these ways in recent years:

1 *Newly Industrializing Countries* (*NICs*).   Singapore; Hong Kong; Taiwan; South Korea; Mexico; Brazil.

2 *OPEC* (*Organization of Petroleum Exporting Countries*). Iraq; Kuwait; Iran; Qatar; Saudi Arabia; United Arab Emirates; Venezuela; Indonesia; Nigeria; Ecuador; Colombia; Algeria.

These countries have become so much richer as a result that it is perhaps rather misleading to call them 'Third World' countries at all.

Population control

Several governments have become very concerned at the huge increase in their countries' populations. Birth control clinics have been set up to advise people about various methods. However, we have already seen (p. 102) that many people in poor countries want to have a lot of children. The problem then is how to persuade them otherwise. In India a great deal of publicity, especially by posters, has been done to show people the advantages of small families. But suppose persuasion does not work? Are people to be *forced* not to have children? Anthony Burgess in his novel, *The Wanting Seed* (1962), has shown what might happen if Britain became seriously over-populated. Here is a conversation between two of the main characters; Tristram, a teacher, and Beatrice-Joanna, who has just discovered that she is pregnant.

‘ ‘However it happened,’ he said, sitting, ‘you'll have to get rid of it. You'll have to take something. You won't want to leave it till you have to go to the Abortion Centre. That'll be shameful. That'll be almost as bad as breaking the law. Carelessness,’ he muttered. ‘No self-control.’

‘Oh, I don't know.’ She was too cool about the whole thing. ‘Things may not be as bad as you think. I mean, people have been having children in excess of the ration and nothing much has happened to them. . . .’

‘Look,’ he said. ‘The days of asking are over. The state doesn't ask any more. The State orders, the State compels. Do you realize that in China people have actually been put to death for disobeying the birth-control laws? Executed. Hanged or shot – I'm not sure which. It's in a letter I got from Emma.’

‘This isn't China,’ she said. ‘We're more civilized here.’

‘Ah, arrant bloody nonsense. It's going to be the same everywhere. The parents of one of my pupils were carted off by the Population Police – do you realize that? It happened only last night. And, as far as I can gather, they hadn't even had the baby yet. She just happened to be pregnant, as far as I can gather.’ ’

The reference to China is interesting because by the early 1980s China did in fact try to make large families illegal. People who had too many children have not been executed, but they have been punished by imprisonment.

How can conditions be improved?

Government posters encouraging people to use birth control. The recommended number of children in India and Africa is three. The message on the Indian poster reads: 'After three no more'.

International help

Aid

For many years rich countries have been helping the poor countries in several ways:

1 *Loans.* Money is lent for schemes like dams, irrigation, factories.

2 *Technical experts.* They are sent to help these countries to improve their agriculture and industry.

3 *The World Bank.* This provides loans for development projects. The Bank's funds come from the rich countries.

4 *UN Specialized Agencies.* The money and technical experts used by the UN Specialized Agencies such as FAO and WHO (see p. 44) come mainly from the rich countries.

However, there have been problems with aid programmes. For example, some schemes have been far too grand, when simple projects like village wells would have been better. In some countries there is corruption. As a result politicians and officials take the money and the poor do not benefit. Also, many poor countries are feeling that they do not wish to receive charity: they would gain more from a more just trading system.

The New International Economic Order (NIEO)

Therefore the poor countries have banded together to demand that the system of international trade should be reformed. They believe that the rich countries benefit too much. A few changes have been made (see pp. 115–116).

UN conferences

In order to alert the world to some of the serious problems mentioned in this chapter, the United Nations has organized a number of conferences, for example:

1 World Population Conference, 1974.

2 Conference on Human Settlements, 1976.

3 United Nations Conference on Trade and Development (UNCTAD). This has been the most important and has met several times since it was first set up in 1964 (see pp. 115–116).

The Committee and the Report

By the later 1970s many people had reached the view that:

1 The economic relations between the rich and poor countries of the world are unjust.

2 The problems of the world are becoming so serious that disaster is likely unless the rich countries of the north help and cooperate with the poor countries of the south.

In 1977 a group of people from both rich and poor countries started to meet to discuss these problems. Their Chairman was Willy Brandt, a former Chancellor (that is, Prime Minister) of West Germany. They produced a report. It is called *North–South: A Programme for Survival*. It is usually referred to as the *Brandt Report* (see also pp. 98 and 107).

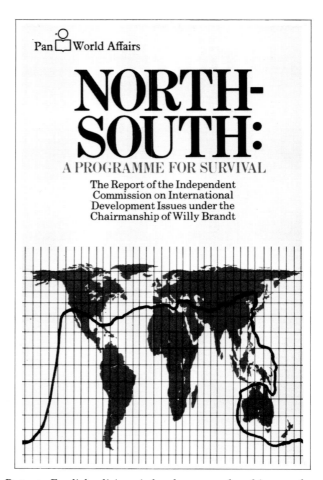

The Brandt Report, English edition: it has been translated into 20 languages

Recommendations of the Brandt Report

The problem

The subtitle of the Report, 'A Programme for Survival' was carefully chosen. This is what the Committee had to say:

‘ The crisis through which international relations and the world economy are now passing presents great dangers, and they appear to be growing more serious. We believe that the gap which separates rich and poor countries – a gap so wide that at the extremes people seem to live in different worlds – has not been sufficiently recognized as a major factor in this crisis . . . we have all come to agree that fundamental changes are essential, whether in trade, finance, energy, or other fields, if we are to avoid a serious breakdown of the world economy in the decades of the eighties and nineties. ’

Recommendations

Detailed advice is given in the report about tackling problems such as food production, over-population and international trade.

The general message is that the rich countries can easily afford to help the poor countries. Also that if they do not, the northern countries will suffer seriously from a breakdown in international trade which is the basis of their wealth. What is more, these changes must be brought about soon – before the end of the century.

What has been done?

Very little. The *Brandt Report* was published in 1980. In 1981 the leaders of the richest countries of the world met at Cancun in Mexico. The USA and Britain refused to do very much to help the poor countries. The other rich countries felt that they could do little without them. Meanwhile, the months are ticking by. . . .

Questions

1 a What do the initials LDC mean?

   b What does 'per capita GNP' mean?

   c What is 'malnutrition'?

   d What are the four main clues to a country's level of poverty?

   e How can the climate of a country cause poverty?

   f Why does over-population sometimes cause poverty?

   g List seven ways in which more food could be made available to poor countries.

   h Name six Newly Industrializing Countries. What continents are they in?

   i How can international aid help poor countries?

   j Why is the subtitle of the *Brandt Report* particularly appropriate?

2 Write an essay or hold a class discussion on why rich countries do not help poor countries more.

3 Study map 8 (below) and calculate which area of the world is growing: (a) the fastest and (b) the slowest.

4 Study maps 2–5 on pp. 95 and 96. List the three countries with: (a) lowest calorie intake; (b) lowest average age of death; (c) lowest per capita GNP; (e) lowest literacy rates. State the continent of each country.

5 Read the following extract and answer the questions.

   ❛ Many hundreds of millions of people in the poorer countries are preoccupied solely with survival and elementary needs. For them work is frequently not available or, when it is, pay is very low and conditions often barely tolerable. Homes are constructed of impermanent materials and have neither piped water nor sanitation. Electricity is a luxury. Health services are thinly spread and in rural areas only rarely within walking distance. Primary schools, where they exist, may be free and not too far away, but children are needed for work and cannot easily be spared for schooling. Permanent insecurity is the condition of the poor. There are no public systems of social security in the event of unemployment, sickness or death of a wage-earner in the family. Flood, drought or disease affecting people or livestock can destroy livelihoods without hope of compensation. In the North, ordinary men and women face genuine economic problems – uncertainty, inflation, the fear if not the reality of unemployment. But they rarely face anything resembling the total deprivation found in the South. ❜

   North-South: A Programme for Survival
   (*The Brandt Report*) (1980)

   a What does 'survival and elementary needs' mean?

   b What is the difference between poverty in the 'North' and the 'South'?

Map 8   Population increase by continent

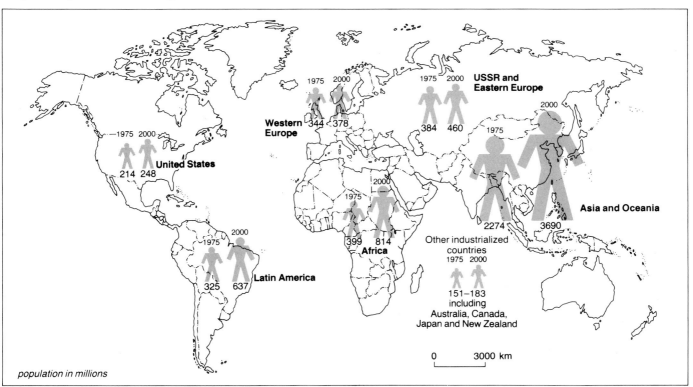

population in millions

8 The international economy

Inflation in Britain, 1968–1984

8.1 Current problems

Balance of payments and debts

Living within one's means

❛ Observe that if a man had twenty pounds a-year for his income, and spent nineteen pound nineteen shillings and sixpence, he would be happy, but if he spent twenty pounds one he would be miserable. ❜

In this way Mr Micawber in Dickens' *David Copperfield* (1849/50) summed up the problem of a family trying to live within its means. A family must arrange its spending so that it does not fall into debt. A family can vary its pattern of spending in two ways:

1 By borrowing; for example by using a mortgage or hire-purchase.

2 By spending money previously saved; for example by drawing out from a bank or building society.

Balance of payments

Countries, just like families, must live within their means. Very few countries are self-sufficient, that is, able to supply themselves with everything they need. And so, in order to buy food or manufactured goods from abroad, a country must sell some of its own products to earn the necessary money.

A country can earn money in a number of different ways:

1 *by selling* – food, raw materials, manufactured goods;

2 *by fees paid* – for services, like banking and insurance, and interest on loans to other countries;

Current problems

3 *by money spent* – in the country by tourists.

Each year a country must add up all that it has spent and all that it has earned. The difference between the two figures is the 'balance of payments'.

If the balance of payments is a 'deficit' figure, that is, if the country has spent more than it has earned, then it must take one or more of the following actions:

1 Live off its savings if the balance of payments has been in credit in previous years.

2 Work harder and earn more by exports in the future.

3 Import less and reduce its standard of living in the future.

4 Borrow money from the International Monetary Fund (IMF)

(see p. 112) or private banks.

Countries in debt

A number of countries have recently built up huge debts – Poland, Mexico, Argentina and Brazil for example (see also fig 2, p. 113). A number of causes have led to debt throughout the world:

1 The huge increases in the cost of oil since the early 1970s (see p. 142).

2 The rise in the number of people unemployed and who are therefore not 'producing wealth' (p. 111).

3 The slump in the price of some products, for example cocoa and sugar.

4 Mismanagement by some governments of the money they

have. For example, even very poor countries have spent a lot on arms.

Inflation

What is inflation?

In recent years many countries in the so-called First and Third Worlds (see chapter 7) have been suffering from inflation, some much more seriously than others. Inflation means the reduction in the value of money. When there is inflation, £1.00 buys less one year than it did in the previous year. For example, from 1978 to 1984 many prices more than doubled: the price of a gallon of petrol rose from about 80p to £1.90; a large sliced white loaf from 26.5p to 33.5p. The cartoon opposite shows the trend.

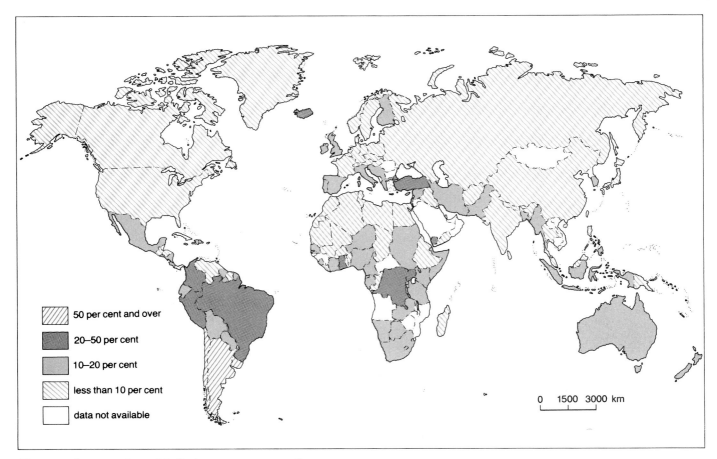

50 per cent and over	
20–50 per cent	
10–20 per cent	
less than 10 per cent	
data not available	

0   1500 3000 km

Map 1   Average Annual inflation rates, 1970–1980

Current problems

Why is inflation bad?

You might think that inflation is not particularly a problem. After all, if wages keep pace with prices, no one suffers. In fact, inflation *is* a problem, especially if the rate becomes too fast. Here are some reasons why:

1 Some groups of people are more successful than others in obtaining higher wages.

2 Unless interest rates can keep pace with inflation, the value of people's savings is reduced.

3 If prices increase more sharply in one country than most others, then that country will find it difficult to export its goods. Either the other countries will not be able to afford them or they will be able to buy similar goods elsewhere more cheaply.

4 'One thing leads to another'. The real fear about inflation is that, once it has started, it is difficult to stop. Higher prices lead to higher wages; higher wages lead to higher prices.

What can be done about it?

No one knows for sure how to cure inflation because no one is absolutely sure what causes it.

There are, of course, some obvious causes. For example, the sudden and huge increase in the price of oil in 1973 (see p. 141) sent many other prices soaring: petrol; electricity (because of oil-fired generators); food (because of transport costs and because artificial fertilizers are made from oil). Obviously, the problem of inflation could be greatly eased if such sudden changes could be avoided.

However, inflation still happens even without such dramatic price rises. Some politicians and economists believe that inflation is

also caused by governments printing too much money. They believe that the way to bring down inflation is for governments to print less money and to arrange for less money to be needed. One of the quickest ways to reduce the flow is to keep wages down and to stop the government itself from spending too much money. This is what Mrs Thatcher tried to do as Prime Minister from 1979. But one of the penalties has been high unemployment.

Unemployment

The size of the problem

Many millions of people in the world are unemployed. Most of these are in the towns and cities of the First and Third Worlds. Communist countries try to ensure that everyone has a job, partly by encouraging labour-intensive jobs, though, as a result, perhaps not everyone does a full day's work.

The number of people out of work is usually given as a percentage of the total working population. For example, in 1984 over 13 people in every 100 in Britain who were available for work were unemployed. But this figure does not, of course, include *everyone* who is affected by unemployment. For many of the unemployed have families to look after. So the families are affected too.

Why is there so much unemployment?

1 Government policies to keep down inflation can lead to unemployment (see above).

2 Changes in industry mean fewer jobs are available. With the coming of automation (see p. 130) many jobs previously done by people in factories are now performed by machines.

3 Increase in population means there are more people than jobs. The huge increase in the population of many Third World countries (see pp. 100–103) has outstripped the creation of new jobs. There is not enough money available to build new factories or create new firms to employ the extra, spare people.

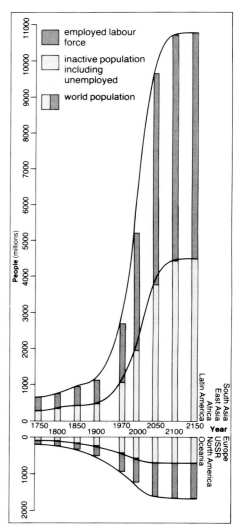

Fig. 1 The estimated numbers of people unemployed, 1750–2150: projected growth in world population and division into employed labour force and inactive population

Current problems

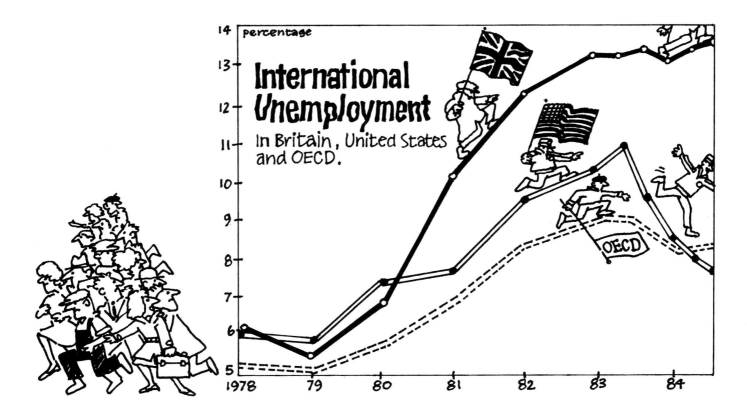

Why is unemployment bad?

1 People who are unemployed become very discontented. They see that it is unjust that some people have work while others, like themselves, do not. Sometimes the discontent is so serious that riots break out (see p. 87).

2 People who are out of work are not creating wealth. Also, if they are living on government unemployment benefit, they are living on the wealth produced by people who *are* in employment and who are paying the taxes for these benefits. It is wasteful and inefficient for a country to have a lot of its able-bodied workforce unemployed.

The problems all together

What is worrying about these problems is that they are all connected. For example, if inflation and unemployment are connected, how do you decide which should be tackled first? There are basically two ways of handling economic matters:

1 Communists plan and regulate as much as they can (see chapter 4).

2 Capitalists believe that individuals and firms work best if allowed the freedom to make profits.

The Capitalist system works well when the amount of wealth being created gradually *increases* from year to year. This is called 'growth'. This happened in the 1960s.

When firms go bankrupt and people are unemployed, the amount of wealth being created *decreases*. This is called 'recession'. This has been happening since the mid-1970s.

There are two main reasons for this:

1 The whole American economy suffered very seriously because of the huge cost of the war in Vietnam from 1960 to 1973. All other non-Communist countries are affected by the condition of America.

2 The great increase in the price of oil, especially in 1973 and 1979.

The fear is that the whole Capitalist system will collapse, causing untold misery and discontent. The greatest crisis occurred in 1929 in the USA when shares suddenly collapsed in value, banks and other companies went out of business, causing mass unemployment and contraction of international trade.

Teletext: exchange rates displayed on Ceefax

Currencies

Exchange rates

If we hand over a £1.00 coin in a shop in Britain, the shopkeeper will know how much it is worth (unless it is forged!), whether the shop is in London, Manchester, Glasgow, Belfast or Swansea. But how much is £1.00 worth in New York, or Paris, or Bombay? The only way to answer that question is to know the 'exchange rate', that is, the equivalent of £1.00 in dollars, francs or rupees. (British currency is sometimes called 'sterling'.)

But who decides what these equivalent values are? For many years each government decided what the value of its currency was and when it was necessary to change it. For example, after the Second World War £1.00 equalled $4.03. Then, in 1949, the British government 'devalued' the pound, that is, they reduced it to $2.80 (see cartoon, right). One of the main reasons for devaluation is to cope with a balance of trade deficit (see p. 109). 'Devaluation' means that a country's exports are cheaper and its imports are dearer.

Since 1972 most non-Communist governments have agreed to let their currencies 'float'. By this arrangement, governments no longer control the values of their currencies. The values vary from day to day and are calculated by the foreign exchanges that handle the flow of money. If people have confidence to invest in a particular currency, there will be demand for it and its value will rise. The exchange rate of the pound for the day in relation to the dollar is often given in that evening's television news bulletins.

The International Monetary Fund (IMF)

If exchange rates fluctuate too wildly, it is difficult to make effective plans for international trade: you will never know quite what your goods are going to be worth in another country! So at the end of the Second World War the International Monetary Fund (IMF) was set up. By 1980, 138 non-Communist countries were members. The purpose of the IMF is to influence exchange rates so as to prevent wild fluctuations.

The IMF arranges loans to countries with balance of payments problems. Some of these loans are in the form of a special international currency called 'Special Drawing Rights' (SDRs). The loans are made on condition that the borrowing country arranges its economy more efficiently, though often countries do not live up to their promises.

Commercial banks

The amount of money lent by the IMF is, in fact, much smaller than the sums provided by private banks. Commercial banks – the ordinary banks in the High Streets – earn money by the interest they charge on loans. Some of the biggest banks in America, Britain and West Germany have lent huge sums of money to other countries.

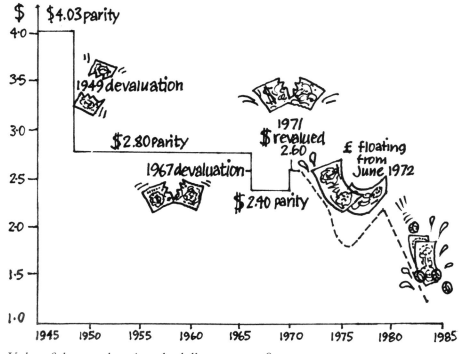

Value of the pound against the dollar, 1945–1985

International finance

By the early 1980s some countries with the biggest debts, such as Poland, Mexico, Argentina and Brazil (see p. 109), were in so much difficulty that they could not even pay the interest let alone make repayments on the 'principal' (that is, the sum borrowed). There are only two possible outcomes, both unpleasant:

1 The debtor countries 'default'. That is, they claim that they are bankrupt and refuse to repay the banks at all. The lending banks could then collapse.

2 The debt is 're-scheduled'. This is a polite word for saying that the debtor can have more time to pay. But it is difficult to see how some countries will *ever* be able to repay all their debts.

The World Bank

The full name of the World Bank is the International Bank for Reconstruction and Development. It was set up at the same time as the IMF (see p. 112), the same countries are members and both are part of the United Nations system (see p. 44). America is by far the biggest contributor of funds, as it is for the IMF.

As the full name of the World Bank shows, it provides money for particular development projects. Most of its business is therefore with Third World countries. Large sums of money have been made available for projects like irrigation, flood control, road construction, building factories. The World Bank also provides expert technical advisers for such projects, as well as the money.

World Bank, Washington: its work includes the International Development Association

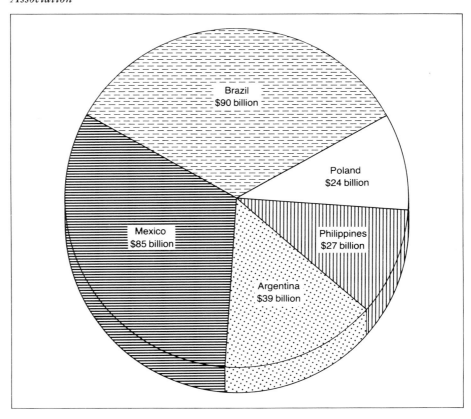

Fig 2 Countries with the largest international debts 1984

8.3 International trade

Free trade and tariffs

Why is international trade important?

There are few countries in the world that are able to produce everything they need. Russia, with its huge, varied lands, could perhaps be a self-sufficient country. But most countries need to buy from others because:

1 The country cannot grow certain food or does not contain certain minerals or metals. For example, it is not possible in Britain to grow bananas, or to mine copper. If we want to eat bananas or use copper in plumbing, we need to import these.

2 The country has not developed the skill to produce certain goods and it is cheaper to import them than to try to compete. For example, Britain does not make long-range airliners but buys them from America.

International trade makes it possible for people to have and use goods that would otherwise not be available in certain countries.

How is trade sometimes hindered?

Generally speaking everyone benefits from 'free trade'. Free trade is a system in which governments do not place any obstacles in the way of international trading.

But sometimes governments set up barriers. There are three main kinds of restrictions governments use:

1 *Customs duties.* A form of tax on imported goods to contribute to the government's income.

2 *Tariffs.* Duties placed on imports to reduce the amount of imports by making goods dearer.

3 *Quotas.* Limits placed on the numbers or amounts of particular goods allowed to be imported at all.

There are two main reasons why governments sometimes wish to restrict imports (this is called 'protectionism'):

1 To protect a country which is in debt on balance of payments (see pp. 108–109).

2 To protect a particular industry from the competition of similar imported goods.

The General Agreement on Tarriffs and Trade (GATT)

Protectionism is dangerous, for two reasons:

1 It restricts the total amount of world trade. This in turn can lead to increased unemployment.

2 Quarrels over problems of international trade can lead to war.

As part of the United Nations collection of organizations most non-Communist countries have joined the GATT system (see p. 114). Members have agreed to reduce tariffs and quotas. They meet to review the condition of world trade and make arrangements for freer trade.

The most important negotiations have been the 'Kennedy Round' in 1964–67 and the 'Tokyo Round' in 1973–79. The first arranged for large reductions in tariffs on manufactured goods. The second tackled the problem of tariffs on agricultural produce. Since then, however, many countries have been much less willing to give up protectionism.

International trade

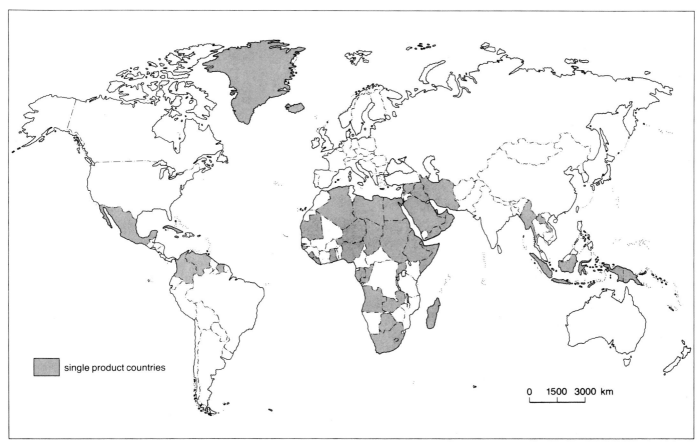

Map 2   Countries dependent upon a single product for more than half their export income, 1980

The New International Economic Order (NIEO)

How is the traditional system unjust?

Most of the countries of the Third World have been colonies of European countries. When the colonies were under European control, the Europeans decided what their colonies should produce and how they should trade. Although the colonies are now politically independent, the old trading systems still continue.

One of the most serious problems is that many Third World countries have come to rely for their foreign income on only one product: for example, Zambia on copper, Ghana on cocoa. The price they can obtain for these exports is fixed by the richer countries. In recent years the prices have dropped and so the Third World countries have suffered.

Actions taken within the United Nations (UN)

During the 1960s, as the colonies became independent they became members of the UN. They joined together to demand a New International Economic Order. At first there were 77 Third World countries making this demand. Although there are now well over 100, they are still called the 'Group of 77'.

The UN recognized that the problem was serious and important.

Two particular actions were taken:

1 *United Nations Conference on Trade and Development (UNCTAD).* In fact, this was not just a temporary gathering for a conference. A permanent office was set up so that UNCTAD has become something like a UN Specialized Agency (see p. 44) dealing with Third World trade and development problems.

2 *First and Second UN Development Decades.* This was the name given to the years 1961–70 and 1971–80. All countries were asked to make a special effort to help the LDCs (see pp. 92 and 98) to improve their standards of living. The First Development Decade was quite successful. However, the Second

International trade

UNCTAD; *formed in 1964, and administered by a Permanent Trade and Development Board*

What reforms do the LDCs want?

1 More trade through assured prices and help to develop several different products for sale.

2 More financial help, especially by having a bigger say in how the IMF conducts its business.

3 Help to modernize, especially to use modern science and technology to develop industries.

4 Setting up of stocks of food to help the really needy.

Trade among the developed countries

Organization for Economic Co-operation and Development (OECD)

Twenty-three rich non-Communist countries are members of the OECD (see map 3). They have meetings to agree on how they can co-operate among themselves and help world trade generally.

Development Decade was a failure because of all the serious problems of the early 1970s already mentioned:
a) Great increase in the price of oil (see p. 142) – this affected the LDCs even more than developed countries.

b) Inflation (see pp. 109–110) – therefore the LDCs had to pay more for their imports.
c) Recession (see p. 111) – therefore the developed countries were buying less from the LDCs.

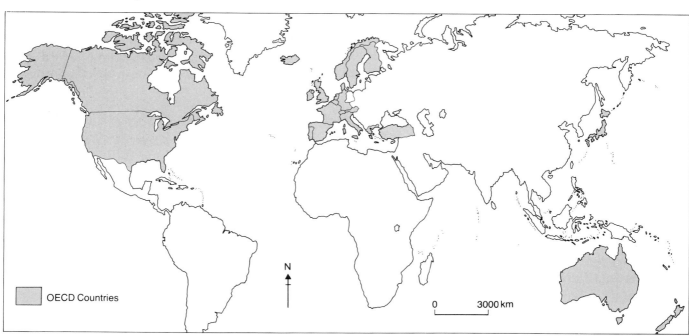

OECD Countries

N

0   3000 km

Map 3   Members of the OECD

International trade

Japan

Many manufactured goods in Britain now are made in Japan, for example; Datsun cars, Nikon cameras, Sony televisions. Japan has increased her wealth by an increase in trade. The cartoon (right) shows just how successful the Japanese have been.

East–West trade

Because of the Cold War (see p. 56) there is not much trade between the Communist and non-Communist developed countries. However, in recent years there have been four important trading developments:

1 *Russia is importing.* Russian agriculture is so inefficient that she needs to import food. American farmers produce huge surpluses and are therefore pleased to sell grain to Russia.

2 *Loans.* Several Western banks have lent large sums of money to some East European countries,

Increase in Japanese per capita income 1945–1981

especially Poland.

3 *Gas pipeline.* Russia, with the help of European companies, is building a pipeline from Siberia to Western Europe to sell natural gas, especially to West Germany.

4 *Trade with China.* The USA and several European countries have increased trade with China. China is in many ways a Third World country and needs western help in technology and industry.

Japanese goods sold in Britain

International trade

A poster advertising 'Better Made in Britain'; a campaign started in 1984 to encourage people to 'buy British'

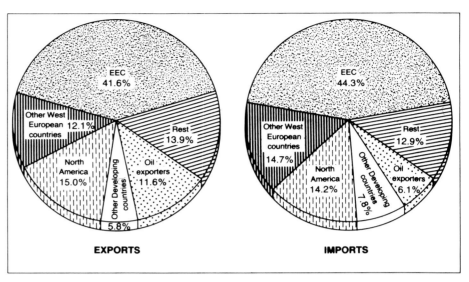

Fig 3   Britain's main trading partners, 1982

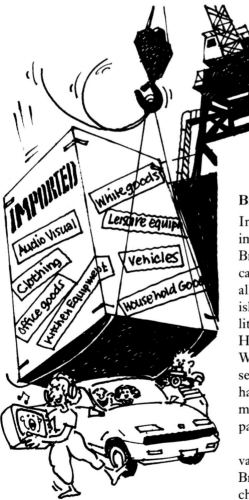

world trade has declined and the amount of imports is increasing. Many of the trends are worrying. That is why the government has coined the slogan, 'Buy British' and more recently, why the campaign, 'Better Made in Britain' has been started.

Britain

International trade is particularly important for Britain. Although Britain's farms are efficient, they cannot produce enough food to feed all the people on the densely-packed island. Britain must therefore literally trade in order to live. However, since the Second World War Britain has found it difficult to sell as much as she would like. She has even been *importing* the kind of manufactured goods she has in the past *exported*.

The graphs and the cartoon show various trends in patterns of trading. Britain's trading partners have been changing, the country's share of total

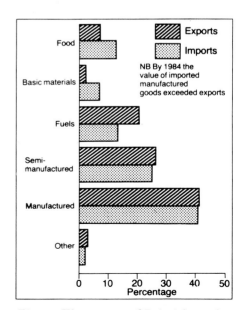

Fig 4   The pattern of Britain's trade, 1982

8.4 Increase in size

Common markets

The European Economic Community (EEC)

Ten countries in Europe now belong to the EEC (the European Economic Community) or what is often called the 'Common Market' (see map 4). It was set up in 1957. Many complaints are made about it. For example, Britain has complained that regulations about fishing have harmed Britain's fishing industry. Britain has also complained that its contribution to the Community budget is unjustly high.

Most serious of all are the problems related to the *Common Agricultural Policy* (CAP). Community farmers are guaranteed prices for their products. As a result, too much of some food has been produced. Large quantities then have to be stored – in 'butter mountains' and 'wine lakes', for example. This policy has put a great strain on the Community's finances.

On the other hand, the Community is quite a remarkable

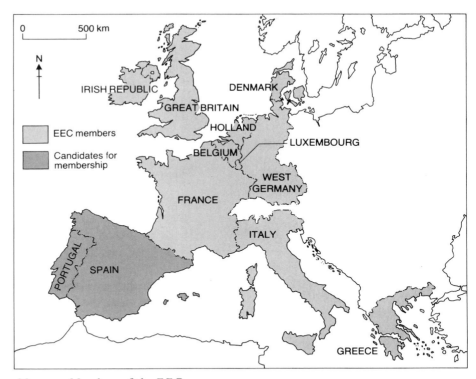

Map 4   Members of the EEC

achievement. No other group of countries have ever come together voluntarily and agreed to combine such large areas of their economies. Why have the European countries done this? There is not space here to describe the complicated history of the European Community. But two important benefits should be noted:

1 *Wealth and power.*   The ten countries can act as a single, large unit in bargaining talks. It is therefore much wealthier and more powerful than any of the individual countries on their own.

2 *'Economy of scale.'*   Trade is very much easier between each of the member-countries than with other countries outside the Community. Firms can therefore make goods to sell to a much larger number of people than just the people of their own country. Once the factory has been built and the tools installed, it is often much more efficient to make a lot of goods rather than a few. This is called 'economy of scale'.

Farmers protest at the French Embassy about unfair competition in the Common Market from French eggs

Increase in size

Other common markets

There are two other important 'common markets' though with more limited co-operation (see map 5):

1 *Comecon.* This is sometimes called the 'Communist Common Market'. 'Comecon' is an abbreviation for 'Council for Mutual Economic Assistance'.

2 *Asean.* This is the non-Communist 'Association of South-East Asian Nations'.

Multinationals

Economies of scale can also be achieved if individual firms set up branches to trade in different countries. This has become quite common in recent years. These huge firms are called 'multinationals' because they operate in several countries. A number of these are so wealthy and sell such huge amounts of their products that they earn more

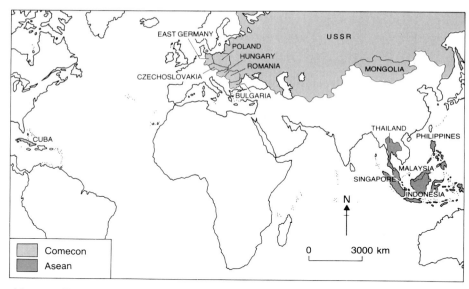

Map 5   Two international economic organizations: Comecon and Asean

money in a year than the GNP (see p. 93) of many of the smaller countries of the world (see map 6, below). Some of the more famous multinational companies are:

1 Exxon (or Esso) the oil firm;

2 IBM (International Business Machines) the computer firm;

3 ICI (Imperial Chemical Industries) the chemical firm;

4 ITT (International Telephone and Telecommunications) the telephone and telex firm.

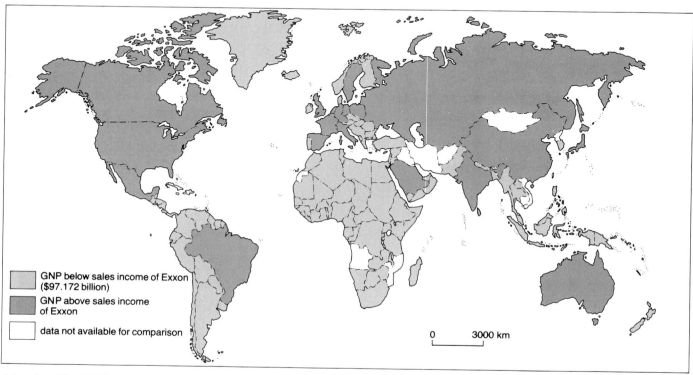

Map 6   The GNP of countries compared with the sales income of the multinational oil company, Exxon, 1981–2

Questions

1 a List three main ways in which a country can earn money.
 b Give three reasons why countries get into debt.
 c Explain the meaning of the word 'inflation'. Why do you think it is dangerous?
 d What do the following mean? (i) 'balance of payments'; (ii) 'deficit figure'; (iii) 'exchange rate'; (iv) 'floating currency'.
 e What is the difference between the World Bank and the IMF?
 f What is 'protectionism'?
 g What do the following initials mean? (i) GATT; (ii) UNCTAD; (iii) OECD; (iv) EEC; (e) CAP.
 h What were the four main reforms in the international economic system demanded by the Least Developed Countries (LDCs)?
 i Is there any trade between the Communist and non-Communist developed countries?
 j How many countries are now members of the EEC?
 k What do the following initials mean? What kind of organizations are they? (i) IBM; (ii) ICI; (iii) ITT.

2 Look around your home and list as many items as possible which have been imported.

3 Read the following extract and answer the questions.

❝ THE VICTIMS of any trade war will be the workers of the world. More than 300 million of them have no job or can only scrape a bare subsistence, says the International Labour Organization.

A beggar-thy-neighbour policy of protectionism would condemn more millions to the scrap heap.

But the pressure for import controls – as a desperate way to save jobs – is growing stronger among the trade unions of the industrialized west.

In the advanced nations of the Organisation for Economic Co-operation and Development (OECD) more than 5 per cent are now jobless, a figure not reached since the grim days of the early thirties.

A forthcoming OECD report will argue that unemployment can no longer be treated as a temporary halt in the onward march of progress in the affluent part of the world.

It is that startling suddenness of the return of unemployment that mystifies economists and politicians alike.

In 1973 there were around 2.5 million jobless in the European Economic Community; five years later the average totals more than six million.

Over the same period unemployment in the United States rose from 4.3 million to just under 7 million and in Japan from 680,000 to 1.1 million. In 1970 the West Germans had less than 100,000 on the dole; now the total is more than a million. ❞

The Guardian, 1978

 a Draw a graph to compare the increase in unemployment from 1973 to 1978 for the countries mentioned.
 b Why do you think that 'pressure for import controls is growing stronger among trade unions', if such a policy 'would condemn more millions to the scrap heap'?

5 Look at the cartoon (below) and answer the questions.
 a Who is the snoozing male character?
 b What is the message being conveyed by the cartoonist?
 c Why do you think the cartoon was drawn in the first place?

The tide's coming in...and time's running out!

'British European', September 1970

9.1 The importance of technology

Great changes

The speed of change

Inventions like the car, aeroplane, telephone, radio, television and computer have all been developed during the last 100 years. In the richer countries of the northern half of the world these developments have brought great changes to people's lives. Just imagine business or everyday life without these inventions.

What has been particularly remarkable is the great speed with which changes have happened. Never before in history have so many changes in the style and quality of life happened in such a short space of time. Most of these changes have been brought about by technology.

What is 'technology'?

'Technology' is applied science. Theoretical ideas in mathematics, physics and chemistry are used to invent new machines and products and to improve the methods of production. Take, for example, the production of a modern car. It uses the following basic inventions:

1 *Internal combustion engine.* The use of power from an explosive mixture of petrol and air to turn the wheels.

2 *Assembly line.* The subdivision of car construction so that one job is completed at one place in the factory.

3 *Robots.* All the movements and actions necessary to complete the assembly line jobs are done by machines instead of people.

Scientists and engineers

The application of science to industry depends on the education and work of scientists and engineers. There has been such a huge increase in the number of scientists, for example, that it is estimated that 90% of all scientists who have ever lived are alive today! As you can see from map 1, most scientists and engineers are in the rich countries. In the 'Third World' India is the leading nation in the field of scientific research.

11–100 per cent

0–10 per cent

data not available

0   1500   3000 km

Map 1   Proportion of scientists and engineers in the workforce, late 1970s and early 1980s

9.2 Travel

Speed of travel

Two hundred years ago, travel by land depended upon the horse, and travel by water, upon the sailing boat. There was no travel by air. Few people could travel unless they were rich. Great distances took a long time. For example, 200 years ago it took four months to travel by ship from Britain to Australia; it now takes about 26 hours by aeroplane!

Cars

Great numbers of cars are being produced and used in the rich countries of North America, Western Europe, Japan and Australasia. For example, it has been calculated that there were 362 million cars in the world in 1981. Forty per cent of these were owned by Americans. One hundred thousand new cars were being produced each day. It has even become quite common in some rich countries for families to own more than one car.

Thousands of car parks have been made in Britain since about 1960

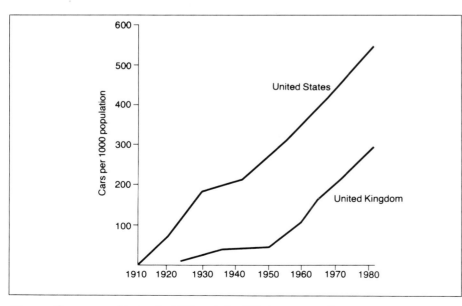

Fig 1   Car ownership in the UK and the USA, 1910–1982

This great increase in car ownership, especially since about 1960, has been made possible by cheap mass production methods. The American car manufacturer, Henry Ford, first developed these methods. He once said, 'You can buy a Ford car in any colour so long as it is black.' It is obviously cheaper to paint cars on a production line just one colour rather than a variety of colours. More recently the cost of wages has been reduced by replacing workers by machines. For example, Fiat advertised their 'Strada' car as being 'hand made by robots' (see also p. 130).

Travel

In rich countries where people can afford cars they have, of course, had a great influence on ways and places of working, shopping and enjoying leisure. Also great areas of land have been taken to build roads. Another effect of cars is road accidents. Even in Third World countries now, as cars become more common, road accidents account for many deaths.

Aeroplanes

The effects of flight

Aeroplanes were developed as recently as the beginning of this century. The first powered flight by the Wright brothers was in 1903. Aeroplanes have had an enormous effect upon travel for two reasons:

1 They can reach much faster speeds than land or sea travel;

2 seas, rivers and mountains are barriers for trains, for example, but they do not affect aeroplanes.

Aeroplanes have also had a great effect on warfare. When armies and navies fight, often only comparatively small areas of countries are affected by the fighting. Because aeroplanes can fly long distances over land and sea, they can bomb any part of an enemy's country. In modern wars, therefore, since the 1930s, civilians have been killed and wounded by attacks from the air. The invention of the aeroplane has meant that civilians are now as likely to be killed in a war as soldiers, sailors and airmen (see drawing above).

Air travel

The main uses for aeroplanes in peacetime are as airliners. Many people now travel on business and pleasure over long distances which would have been almost impossible at the beginning of the century.

One hundred and fifty years ago,

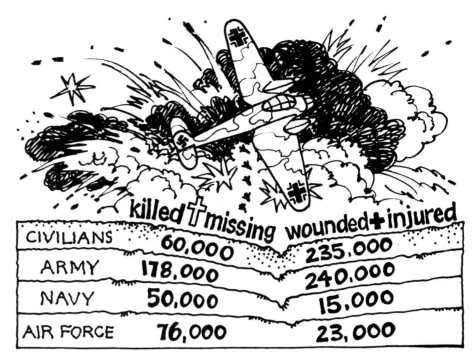

	killed + missing	wounded + injured
CIVILIANS	60,000	235,000
ARMY	178,000	240,000
NAVY	50,000	15,000
AIR FORCE	76,000	23,000

British casualties, 1939–45. Note the number of civilians killed

Heathrow airport. Plans for a third London airport to relieve Heathrow have met with opposition

for example, the British politician, Sir Robert Peel, was on holiday in Rome when the government in London resigned. He had to rush back to London as quickly as possible in order to become the next Prime Minister. It took him a fortnight! Just think how frequently politicians from all over the world now meet for conferences.

Britain is particularly affected by air travel because of her geographical position, and Heathrow is the busiest airport in the world.

Travel

Space exploration

People in space

Very few parts of our planet, Earth, remain to be explored. Now that we have powerful rockets, we have started to explore the Moon, and other planets. The first man-made object to be put into orbit round the Earth was the Russian satellite, *Sputnik I* in 1957 (see p. 129).

The first man in space was the Russian, Yuri Gagarin, in 1961. The first woman in space was also Russian – Valentina Tereshkova in 1963. Then, in 1969, the first men, Americans, landed on the Moon. In 1973 *Skylab* was launched. Three men lived in this spacecraft, circling the Earth, for several months. The dates of these events are not so much important in themselves as indications of the great speed at which progress was made after the first satellite.

Exploring the planets

The Moon is, of course, very close to Earth compared with even the nearest planets: a two-day journey compared with several months to reach Mars or Venus. It is unlikely that journeys to the planets will be made by man for many years yet. However, un-manned spacecraft have been launched to send back close-up pictures of Mars, Venus, Jupiter and Saturn.

Valentina Tereshkova

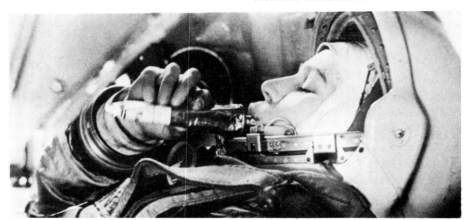

9.3 Communications

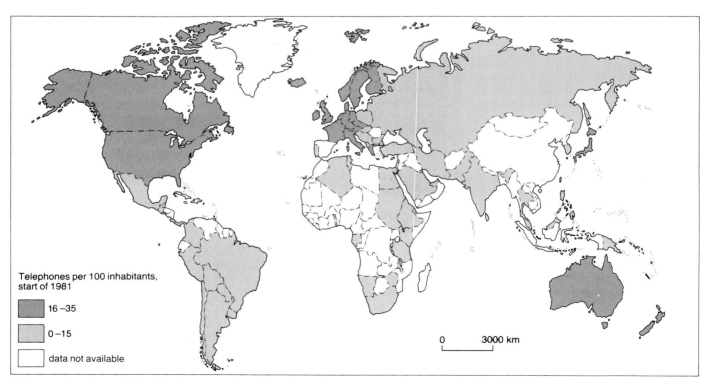

Telephones per 100 inhabitants, start of 1981

16 – 35

0 – 15

data not available

0   3000 km

Map 2   Numbers of telephones per 100 people, early 1981

Communications

The technological complexity of telephone systems. British Telecom was privatized in 1984: its shares were sold for £4 billion

Telephone

In the home

If people are not able or do not wish to travel, they can speak to each other by telephone. In recent years there has been a huge increase in the number of telephones in use in the richer countries (see map 2). For example, by 1980 it was estimated that in Britain alone 17 000 000 000 telephone calls were being made in a year. It is, of course, very convenient to have a telephone – for emergencies, shopping and just 'keeping in touch'.

By using computers (see pp. 130–132) it is now possible to dial direct to many millions of other telephones, including those in countries thousands of miles away. By using satellites (see p. 129) the voices of people in distant countries are very clear.

Telephones for business and politics

An enormous amount of business is now settled by telephone. Many big firms and organizations have telex machines. These produce printed sheets of information from telephone messages.

It is sometimes important for politicians, like Presidents and Prime Ministers, to speak to each other urgently by telephone. The most important and famous of these telephone links is the 'hot-line' which enables the American and Russian leaders to communicate with each other if an emergency seems likely to lead to nuclear war (see also p. 19).

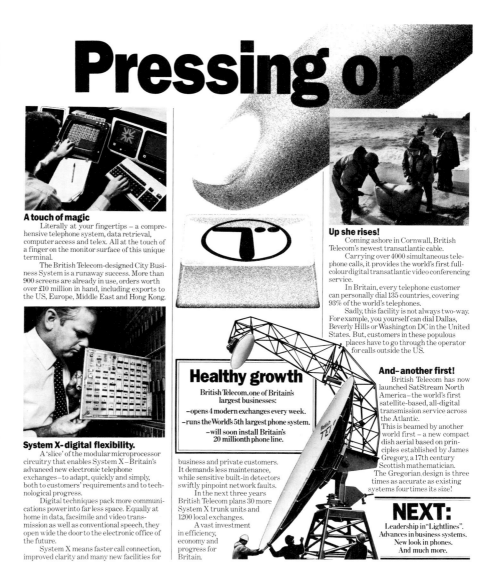

Pressing on

A touch of magic
Literally at your fingertips – a comprehensive telephone system, data retrieval, computer access and telex. All at the touch of a finger on the monitor surface of this unique terminal.
The British Telecom-designed City Business System is a runaway success. More than 900 screens are already in use, orders worth over £10 million in hand, including exports to the US, Europe, Middle East and Hong Kong.

System X- digital flexibility.
A 'slice' of the modular microprocessor circuitry that enables System X – Britain's advanced new electronic telephone exchanges – to adapt, quickly and simply, both to customers' requirements and to technological progress.
Digital techniques pack more communications power into far less space. Equally at home in data, facsimile and video transmission as well as conventional speech, they open wide the door to the electronic office of the future.
System X means faster call connection, improved clarity and many new facilities for

Healthy growth
British Telecom, one of Britain's largest businesses:
– opens 4 modern exchanges every week.
– runs the World's 5th largest phone system.
– will soon install Britain's 20 millionth phone line.

business and private customers. It demands less maintenance, while sensitive built-in detectors swiftly pinpoint network faults.
In the next three years British Telecom plans 30 more System X trunk units and 1200 local exchanges.
A vast investment in efficiency, economy and progress for Britain.

Up she rises!
Coming ashore in Cornwall, British Telecom's newest transatlantic cable.
Carrying over 4000 simultaneous telephone calls, it provides the world's first full-colour digital transatlantic video conferencing service.
In Britain, every telephone customer can personally dial 135 countries, covering 93% of the world's telephones.
Sadly, this facility is not always two-way. For example, you yourself can dial Dallas, Beverly Hills or Washington DC in the United States. But, customers in these populous places have to go through the operator for calls outside the US.

And- another first!
British Telecom has now launched SatStream North America – the world's first satellite-based, all-digital transmission service across the Atlantic.
This is beamed by another world first – a new compact dish aerial based on principles established by James Gregory, a 17th century Scottish mathematician. The Gregorian design is three times as accurate as existing systems four times its size!

NEXT:
Leadership in "Lightlines".
Advances in business systems.
New look in phones.
And much more.

British **TELECOM** The power behind the button.

Radio and television

Leisure and entertainment

It is quite common now for people even in poor countries, to own radios. And in rich countries most people have televisions. Those of us with radios and televisions tend to take them for granted as sources of entertainment.

Imagine the difficulties and cost of enjoying the full range of music, plays, films, comedy and sport without broadcasting. Television especially has completely changed the ways people spend their leisure time. For example, from the 1930s to the 1950s millions of people in the rich countries visited the cinema each week, some more than once, queuing eagerly to see their favourite film stars. Now only a small number of those cinemas still show films. In recent years video-games and films have become quite common in rich countries.

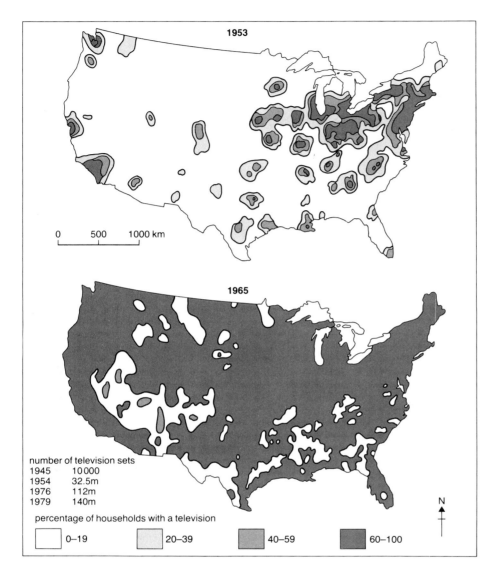

1953

0   500   1000 km

1965

number of television sets
1945   10 000
1954   32.5m
1976   112m
1979   140m

percentage of households with a television

| | 0–19 | | 20–39 | | 40–59 | | 60–100 |

N

Map 3   TV ownership in the USA, 1953–1965

News and education

Radio has been an extremely important source of news in all countries. Listening to the radio is less effort than reading a newspaper. Radios are especially important, of course, in countries where many people are illiterate (see p. 95 and map 5, p. 97). Radio and television have been important ways for political leaders to give messages to their people in times of crisis. Viewing figures in Britain show how people rely on television for news: approximately 20 million watch either the BBC 1 nine o'clock news or ITN's News at Ten.

Radio and television also provide general education. Some programmes are specifically educational, produced for use in schools, for example (see fig 2). In Britain, the Open University allows people to study for degrees with the help of special radio and television programmes. Also, some programmes broadcast for general entertainment have important educational content – for example, nature and travel items.

Most recently, televisions have been adapted so that their screens can show written information like the news. This system is called 'Teletext' (in Britain it is named 'Ceefax' when transmitted by the BBC and 'Oracle' by ITV).

A further development is Viewdata. With this system it is possible to telephone for information

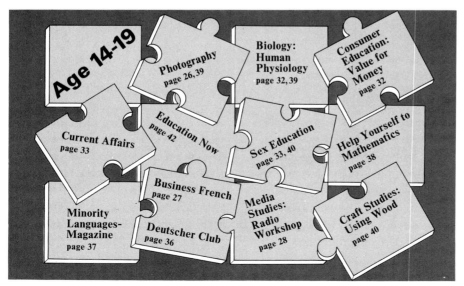

Age 14-19

Photography
page 26, 39

Biology:
Human
Physiology
page 32, 39

Consumer
Education:
Value for
Money
page 32

Current Affairs
page 33

Education Now
page 42

Sex Education
page 33, 40

Help Yourself to
Mathematics
page 38

Business French
page 27

Media
Studies:
Radio
Workshop
page 28

Craft Studies:
Using Wood
page 40

Minority
Languages-
Magazine
page 37

Deutscher Club
page 36

Fig 2   Some of the radio programmes available for schools (based on a BBC pamphlet)

Communications

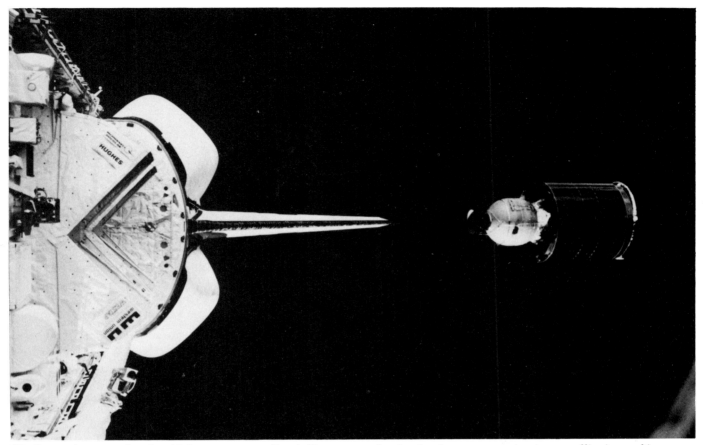

Challenger (a space-shuttle which can return to Earth like an aeroplane) releasing a communications satellite into orbit

to be shown on the television screen. In Britain the Post Office operate a great encyclopaedia of information in this way, called 'Prestel'.

Safety and security

Without radio and (since the 1940s) radar, travelling by ship or aeroplane would be much more dangerous. Radio keeps crews in touch with the world outside their own craft; radar helps them to 'see' in darkness and fog.

Radio and television are also used a great deal by the police. Radios in cars and 'walkie-talkie' radios for police on foot patrol, help policemen to keep in touch with each other and to call in reinforcements. Television cameras also help to guard some shops against thieves.

Satellites

In 1957 the first space vehicle was launched into orbit round the Earth. It was a small Russian satellite called *Sputnik I* and merely carried a radio transmitter. Since then enormous progress has been made in man's exploration and use of space.

'Satellites' are space vehicles that circle round the Earth. Hundreds have been launched. They serve many purposes:

Radio and television

Radio and television signals travel in straight lines. Because the surface of the Earth is curved, it is not possible to send these very great distances. However, it is now possible to 'bounce' them from satellites. By this method it is now possible to watch

television pictures of events many thousands of miles away as they are happening.

Mapping and meteorology

Very accurate photographs can be taken from satellites. The accuracy of maps can be checked; clues about deposits of natural resources can be discovered; and pictures of cloud formations can help in more accurate weather-forecasting.

Military uses

Many of the American and Russian satellites have been placed in orbit for military reasons. They are used for photographing secret military sites like rocket bases. Inventions are even being produced for fighting wars in space with developments like laser beams.

9.4 Machines replace muslces

The first Industrial Revolution

Power

About 200 years ago important changes began to be introduced in Britain, affecting manufacturing and transport. These changes came to be called the Industrial Revolution. Throughout the nineteenth century the same changes happened in America and Europe. They have been happening more recently in Asia and Africa.

One of the most important changes was the replacement of muscle power by machines. First of all, machines were driven by steam. Later oil, petrol and electricity were used. Here are some of the ways in which human and animal muscles have been replaced by machines:

1 Ploughing by tractor instead of horse or ox.

2 Harvesting by combine-harvester instead of sickle and thresher.

3 Land transport by train (steam, electric or diesel), car or bus instead of horse or horse-drawn carriage.

4 Cloth produced in a textile-mill instead of by a weaver.

5 Metal moulded in a foundry instead of by a blacksmith.

Factories

Heavy manufacturing machines need a lot of power to drive them. As a result of the Industrial Revolution many large factories were built where many machines and workers could be collected together. This was because mass production methods (see p. 123) are economical ways of manufacturing.

Silent film actor, Charlie Chaplin, in the film 'Modern Times', 1936: a brilliant satirical commentary on the trends in automation which he foresaw

Automation, cybernetics and computing

What is 'automation' and 'cybernation'?

Since the first Industrial Revolution another wave of change has started to affect industry and our way of life. In this second Industrial Revolution, machines are taking over even more of the work formerly done by people. These changes came in two main stages:

1 *Automation.* In the mechanization of the first Industrial Revolution people have still been needed to operate the machines – by pulling levers or turning wheels, for example. 'Automation' is the next stage. The machines do *all* the work; people are needed just to supervise them – to make them stop, start, speed up, slow down, etc.

2 *Cybernation.* In automation the human brain is still needed to make decisions. The next stage is 'cybernation', when even the human brain is no longer needed. Decisions about the various operations are made by a robot.

Cybernetics is the use of the computer in automation to improve the quality, speed and economy of manufacturing.

Computers and microprocessors

When computers were first built in the 1940s they were large and clumsy machines. Since then it has been found possible to imprint the circuits on tiny, thin wafers of compressed silicon. (Sand consists largely of silicon, so it is very plentiful.) These wafers are called microprocessors or 'microchips'. Even a single chip can do a huge amount of work and carry

Machines replace muscles

a huge amount of information. Also, the speed with which they operate now is down to a billionth of a second for a single operation. Improvements in power, size and speed are being made continuously.

Uses of computers

The computer is not only used in cybernation. It has a very wide range of uses. Here is a recent example, taken from a newspaper report in September 1982:

‘ Big Brother* comes a step nearer. The biggest computer programme in Western Europe was outlined yesterday by the Department of Health and Social Security. Ministers are proposing to invest £700 million in a programme which will involve 70 giant computers, 30 000 terminals and 3000 micro computers. No one will escape being included in the data bank's records. At a touch of a button, local social security clerks will be able to turn up an individual's record immediately on their visual display units. Moreover, unlike the present system, the records of separate departments will be unified – Inland Revenue, DHSS and the Department of Employment. The social security clerk will not only have access to a claimant's sickness record but unemployment and tax records as well. It is easy to see why the Government's critics will be suspicious of yesterday's package not least because of the increase in unemployment it will create – the 117 000 people administrating social security will be cut by up to 25 000. ’
The Guardian, 16 September 1982

(* In his novel, *Nineteen Eighty-Four*, George Orwell described a country where the people are completely controlled by the government, the head of which is called 'Big Brother'.)

A microchip carried by an ant. To show how minute it is, an English black garden ant is about 5 mm long!

A computer game. As computers become cheaper so people in rich countries are buying them to use in their homes

Machines replace muscles

Here are just a few other examples from a huge range of uses for the computer:

1 *Calculations.*
For cash registers in shops; bank accounts; scientific research.

2 *Storing information.*
For police records; warehouse stocks; booking airline seats.

3 *Engineering design.*
For three-dimensional drawings: architecture; cars; aeroplanes.

4 *Manufacture.*
Giving instructions to tools: drilling; cutting; welding.

A training film produced by the Ford car company showing how computers can turn an idea into a fully engineered design

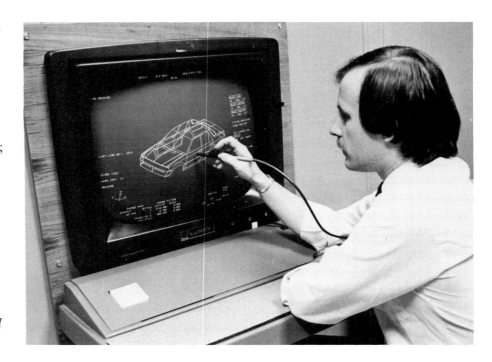

9.5 The effects of technology

Speed

Travelling by aeroplane is much faster than by horse; communicating by telephone is much faster than by letter; calculating complicated sets of figures is much faster by computer than by pencil and paper. The pace of life has speeded up because of technology.

As a result people who can afford these inventions can do more in their lifetimes than they could have done, say, 100 years ago. Also, changes happen much more quickly than in the past. Just think of all the changes brought about by technology that have been experienced by people born at the beginning of this century. People still alive in Britain today lived their childhood years especially if they lived in a village, without seeing a car, an aeroplane, a telephone, a radio, a television, a refrigerator, a record-player, probably not even a gas or electric cooker, or an electric-light bulb!

Work and wealth

Technology has increased enormously the wealth of those countries which have benefited from the inventions. The standard of living of the majority of people in Britain today, for example, is far higher than it was 100 years ago. It is also much higher than that of the majority of people in the Third World countries today.

But not everything has been improved by technology. Technology has also led to unemployment. Because of the great number of changes brought about by technology, some jobs cease to exist and people become unemployed. Since the late 1970s unemployment has become a serious problem in the older industrialized countries like Britain, Belgium and the USA. There are several reasons for this, but one reason is that fewer people are needed when factories become automated. It is possible that because so much wealth can be created by using microchips, countries will be able to employ an increasing proportion of their people in what are called 'service industries'. In other words, instead of people being unemployed, they might be used in entertainment, education, health services, for example. Japan is already developing in this way.

The effects of technology

Problems and alternatives

Resource depletion and pollution

Much of modern technology uses up the resources of the planet, like oil, for instance. Also, the waste products of some industries are dangerous, like radioactive waste from nuclear power-stations, for instance. These problems are discussed in Chapter 10. Some people believe that these bad side-effects of modern technology outweigh its advantages.

The needs of poor countries

In any case, many Third World countries cannot afford some of the expensive inventions of modern technology. For example, it would be quite impossible for the government of India to plan that every family should have a car. Poor countries want the benefits of modern engineering skills but adapted to their more basic needs – for example, pumps for irrigation.

Some examples

Modern technology presents three major problems:

   1 it exhausts the earth's resources;

   2 it pollutes the environment;

   3 it is too expensive for many countries.

   Therefore some engineers have turned their attention to simpler inventions to avoid these problems.

Alternative technology

Most thought has been given to alternative sources of power because the earth's supplies of oil are being used up and nuclear power is so dangerous. Windmills are again being used to convert the force of the wind into usable energy. Solar panels are being produced to convert and store the energy of the sun. Attempts are also being made to try to harness the power of the tides, although this is very difficult. Airships are being developed to replace some aeroplanes; and electrical engines to replace petrol engines in cars. In addition the general ideas of alternative technology are being used to reduce the use of artificial fertilizer in food production and of artificial drugs in medicine.

   Alternative technology is in many ways a return to traditional methods, but with slight improvements adapted from modern scientific knowledge. We are coming to learn that it is unwise to be constantly throwing away old and well-tried ways.

Five-metre square solar panels on these 100-year old London houses heat water for kitchen sinks and baths, March–October

Questions

1 a What percentage of the world's cars are owned by Americans?

   b What effect have aeroplanes had on warfare?

   c What is the busiest airport in the world?

   d Why is Yuri Gagarin famous?

   e What is the 'hot-line'?

   f What are 'Ceefax' and 'Oracle'?

   g What is a 'satellite'? Give three main uses of satellites.

   h What is 'automation' and 'cybernation'?

   i What is meant by 'Big Brother'?

   j What are the problems caused by technology? Give three examples of 'alternative technology'.

2 Write an essay or hold a class discussion on how the microchip is already affecting our lives today.

3 Write an essay or hold a class discussion on the advantages, or disadvantages of 'alternative technology'.

4 Read the following passage and answer the questions.

‘ IN THE THREE short decades between now and the twenty-first century, millions of ordinary, psychologically normal people will face an abrupt collision with the future. Citizens of the world's richest and most technically advanced nations, many of them, will find it increasingly painful to keep up with the incessant demand for change that characterizes our time. For them, the future will have arrived too soon. . . .

Western society for the past 300 years has been caught up in a fire storm of change. This storm, far from abating, now appears to be gathering force. Change sweeps through the highly industrialized countries with waves of ever-accelerating speed and unprecedented impact. It spawns in its wake all sorts of curious social flora – from psychedelic churches and 'free universities' to science cities in the Arctic and wife-swap clubs in California. . . .

Much that now strikes us as incomprehensible would be far less so if we took a fresh look at the racing rate of change that makes reality seem, sometimes, like a kaleidoscope run wild. For the acceleration of change does not merely buffet industries or nations. It is a concrete force that reaches deep into our personal lives, compels us to act out new roles, and confronts us with the danger of a new and powerfully upsetting psychological disease. This new disease can be called 'future shock', and a knowledge of its sources and symptoms helps explain many things that otherwise defy rational analysis. . . .

Behind such prodigious economic facts lies that great, growling engine of change – technology. This is not to say that technology is the only source of change in society. Social upheavals can be touched off by a change in the chemical composition of the atmosphere, by alterations in climate, by changes in fertility, and many other factors. Yet technology is indisputably a major force behind the accelerative thrust.

To most people, the term technology conjures up images of smoky steel mills or clanking machines. This symbol, however, has always been inadequate, indeed, misleading, for technology has always been more than factories and machines. . . .

The old symbols of technology are even more misleading today, when the most advanced technological processes are carried out far from assembly lines or open hearths. Indeed, in electronics, in space technology, in most of the new industries, relative silence and clean surroundings are characteristic – even sometimes essential. And the assembly line – the organization of armies of men to carry out simple repetitive functions – is an anachronism. It is time for our symbols of technology to change – to catch up with the quickening changes in technology itself. ’

Alvin Toffler, *Future Shock* (1971)

   a Explain what the author means by the phrase 'future shock' (line 25).

   b How does technology contribute to the speed of change?

   c Explain the meaning of the following words: (i) 'unprecedented' (line 13); (ii) 'anachronism' (line 47).

   d Do you think that the author approves of change?

5 List three advantages and three disadvantages of the following methods of transport shown in the cartoon below.

10 Resources, conservation, pollution

10.1 Ecology

Our only earth

Earth is quite a small planet. It is the only planet in our solar system that sustains life. Life can exist only on the thin surface of earth and water and its surrounding atmosphere. We should therefore take good care of it. In recent years some people have started to worry; are we taking enough care?

Life forms and the environment are connected and balanced in a complicated and delicate way. This interconnected system is called the 'eco-system'. The study of the interconnections is called 'ecology'.

Strains on the eco-system

Life has existed on earth for billions of years. Yet only in the last few decades has one species, Man, seriously endangered the eco-system. Why is this? There are two main reasons:

The population explosion

As we saw on pp. 100–103, the population of the world is expanding very fast. As a result, more land is needed for growing food, more land is used for building, forests are cleared for timber, firewood and agricultural land.

Industrialization

As we saw on pp. 130–132, technology has increased industrial production enormously. Industry is using up huge quantities of the earth's resources such as metals, and oil and natural gas for energy. Its waste products also cause pollution.

Scientists now understand quite well the dangers we are facing. But it is an extremely difficult political problem. It is hard for governments to take decisions and make agreements which would help to relieve the strains. It is easier and more popular to make short-term decisions than to make big long-term plans.

Ecology

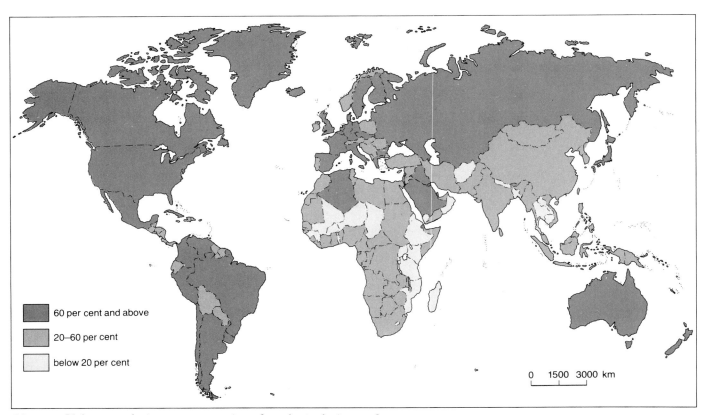

Map 1   Urban population as a proportion of total population, 1980

60 per cent and above

20–60 per cent

below 20 per cent

0   1500   3000 km

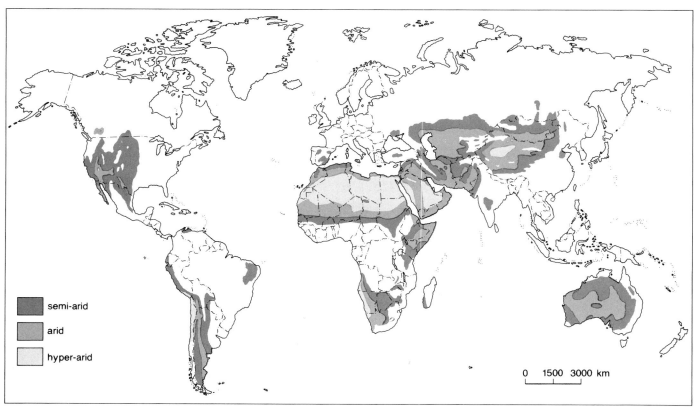

Map 2   The world's deserts

semi-arid

arid

hyper-arid

0   1500   3000 km

Ecology

How is the eco-system in danger?

Pollution

The killing of plants and animals by poisonous wastes (see pp. 144–145).

Resource depletion

The exhaustion of the earth's mineral and energy resources (see pp. 140–143).

Urbanization

During this century large areas of land have been used for building towns and roads. For example, in Russia alone 900 new cities were built between the two World Wars. By the end of the century it is estimated that more people in the world might be living in towns and cities than in the countryside. The more towns and roads that are built the less land there is left for agriculture, forests and wildlife.

Destruction of the land

The layer of fertile soil upon which plants can grow is really very thin. It can easily become exhausted and the land turn to desert. The destruction of the land has three main causes:

  1 Climatic change;

  2 destruction of the habitat: for example if the protecting trees are destroyed;

  3 over-farming.

Much of Northern Africa is now sandy desert, but 2000 years ago it was the main supplier of wheat for the Roman Empire. Today 3.5 million square miles of North and West Africa are desert – the Sahara. And the desert has now started to advance southwards as the Sahel region of Africa becomes a wilderness. Throughout the world it is estimated that by the year 2000 there will be 60% more desert than at present (see map 2).

Deforestation

One of the most serious problems facing the world today is the destruction of the forests, especially the great Amazonian forest in South America. It is estimated that by 2000 the world will have 17% less forest than at present. Why are trees chopped down in such large quantities?

  1 For firewood;

  2 for timber – for building and furniture;

  3 to clear the land for agriculture;

  4 for making paper.

But chopping down so many trees causes serious problems because:

  1 Deforestation can lead to the land becoming desert.

  2 Trees are needed to keep the atmosphere supplied with oxygen, which is necessary for all life.

  3 The forests contain important animals and plants.

This newspaper article explains the seriousness of the problem:

❛ The poorest half of the world's population, two billion people, depends almost entirely on firewood for fuel . . .

As population increases and as the rising cost of other fuels drives even those who could pay for them back to firewood, trees are being chopped down faster than they grow . . .

One hundred million people can no longer get firewood at all. Another billion face shortages. Within 20 years, two and a half billion will not be able to get enough wood to cook their food.

As the trees near the settlements disappear, the women have to trudge further afield . . .

As the trees go, too, the land becomes poorer, the people collect dung and food wastes for fuel, impoverishing the land even more. The top soil blows away leaving a desert . . .

Within 20 years, if nothing changes, one-third of the world's arable land will have turned to dust. ❜

Destruction of species

Largely because of deforestation many species of animals and plants are becoming extinct at an alarming rate. One estimate suggested that as many as 20% of all species in the world at present will be extinct by the year 2000. It is difficult to know what the effects of this will be. One danger is that important sources of medicines, most of which came originally from plants in the wild, will be lost.

Deforestation. Almost half the tropical rain forests of the world have been lost, the rest are dying at a rate of 100 acres a minute

10.2 Food

The problems of supply

In theory it would be possible to feed all the people in the world quite adequately, even with the increased numbers expected in the early part of the next century. But there are a number of problems (see pp. 100–103):

1 Only about 25% of the earth's land surface can be cultivated.

2 Efficient farming is not possible in many poor countries. They need more money for irrigation, pest control, fertilizer, and better tools.

3 It is in the poor countries that population is increasing very rapidly. Yet they cannot increase their food production to keep pace (see p. 103).

4 Rich countries like America produce huge surpluses of food. Even in some poor countries of Africa and Asia there are parts where plentiful food is grown. But it is supplying the needy with this food that is difficult. This is partly because of money, and partly because of difficulties of transport.

Aeroplanes are used for crop-spraying over large areas especially in America

New and improved sources of food

Because of all these problems relating to the supply of food, scientists have developed a number of ways to increase the amount of food produced.

Increase in yields

Sometimes the methods used by farmers are not very efficient. Improving the amount of food produced in proportion to the effort put into the farming is called 'increasing the yield'. This can be done in various ways:

1 *Pest control.* Great quantities of food are eaten by pests. Insects eat grain while it is growing. Rodents (such as rats) and insects (such as weevils) eat food while it is in store. Crop-spraying is now very common; fields of grain plants are dusted with insecticides.

2 *Fertilizer.* Plants will grow more plentifully if the soil is enriched with fertilizer. Animal manure is supplemented by artificial fertilizer.

3 *Selective breeding.* Both plants and animals are being carefully bred

so that strains with the highest food yield are produced. In many poor countries of the world there has been a 'Green Revolution'. A combination of irrigation, fertilizer and high-yield crops has increased the amount of food substantially.

4 *Factory farming.* Large numbers of animals are kept in a small area and are fed mechanically. Battery-chickens are the most common example. Fish-farming is also becoming increasingly common.

New sources of food

Another way of increasing food supply is to develop new forms that have rarely if ever been used before.

1 Most important is the increased use of soya beans. Meat is a very inefficient form of food because animals need to eat so much to produce the meat. Soya is now being flavoured and textured to taste like meat. It is nutritious and, when used as mince, for example, it is almost indistinguishable from meat.

2 New sources of protein are being made from simple organisms like yeast. These are mainly used for animal feed.

Food

Problems

Yet even these various methods of increasing food production have their problems:

1 Insecticides, like DDT, are poisonous not only to insects but also to other animals. If poisoned insects are eaten by one animal, the poison can be passed on through several animals over a wide area. DDT has even been found in penguins in the Antarctic!

2 Certain insects have become resistant to some pesticides and so are therefore no longer killed by them.

3 Fertilizer can trickle into rivers and water supplies, causing pollution.

4 Some artificial fertilizers can exhaust the soil and turn the earth to dust.

5 Factory farming is thought by some to be cruel to the animals.

Chickens are bred in large numbers: eggs are hatched in vast incubators, then the chicks, as here, are packed and fed in a brooder

10.3 Minerals and fuels

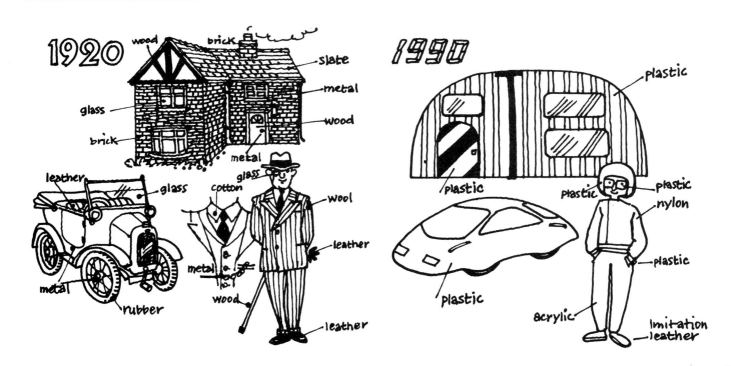

Minerals and fuels

A 'bottle-bank' – used to recycle glass

The problem of forecasting

A number of calculations have been made which show that the earth's supplies of certain very important minerals and fuels will be used up by the beginning of the next century. These include oil and natural gas, which we shall discuss separately later. The list also includes: gold, copper, mercury, lead, tin and zinc. All these are important metals.

On the other hand, some people now believe that these estimates are too pessimistic, for several reasons.

Technology

As prices increase with scarcity, and technology improves, it will be economical to mine and drill for the more difficult deposits. It will be possible to extract some minerals from the sea-bed for example. Oil and gas of course are already obtained in this way.

Recycling

Instead of destroying used or worn-out items, materials can be salvaged. A large proportion of lead is reused already. Recently, in Britain, 'bottle-banks' have appeared on pavements in towns so that glass can be collected, melted down and reused.

Substitutes

Alternatives can be found that are either more plentiful or cheaper. Increasing numbers of man-made materials (chemically known as 'polymers') are replacing natural materials. For example, plastics are replacing wood, glass, brick, metal, rubber, leather, etc. (see cartoon on p. 139); electricity is being generated by nuclear instead of oil-fired power stations.

Oil

Fossil fuels

The coal, oil and natural gas that we extract from the earth are the remains of plants and creatures which died about 300 million years ago. By their very nature, therefore, they cannot be replaced. Coal is still very plentiful, especially in the northern hemisphere. But oil is both much more useful and much less plentiful. So the question of future oil supplies is very important.

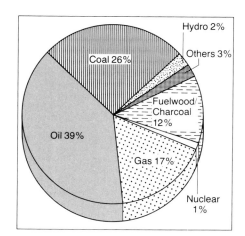

Fig 1   World energy consumption, 1980

The uses of oil

Oil has so many uses it is difficult to imagine life in the richer countries without it.

The two most obvious uses are as:

1 *Fuels and lubricants.* Cars, aeroplanes, tractors, tanks, lorries, most ships, most electricity generating stations, and much central heating all depend on oil.

2 *The basis for many artificial products* – plastics, fertilizers, detergents, inks and insecticides, for example.

A French expert has noted the effects of a world without oil:

❛ Almost all plastics and artificial fibres would disappear. No more nylon, no more ballpoint pens, no more shirts, no more waterproof clothes, no more mothproof woollens, no more records. In modern offices, everything is made of oil – from the carpeting to the dials on telephones, from the wall coverings to the painted metal furniture, from wastebaskets to electric fans. ❜

(Not all of this is entirely true, of course, because other materials can be used, for example cotton for shirts.)

Minerals and fuels

Oil production (billions of barrels per annum). NB 10% decline, 1979–1981

Increase in oil production and consumption

There has been an enormous increase in the use of oil during this century. Production has risen particularly steeply in recent decades – trebling, 1960–80, from roughly one to three billion tonnes per annum.

Some of the biggest commercial companies in the world are oil companies – huge multinational companies such as Esso, Shell and BP. Great tankers ship the crude oil from the oil fields to refineries all over the world. Industrial countries like Japan, West Germany and France, which have no oil supplies of their own, are utterly dependent on these supplies. Britain is extremely lucky to be able to drill for oil in the North Sea. This North Sea oil has made her less worried about supplies from overseas; she would also be a much poorer country if she had to buy a lot of oil from abroad.

Organization of Petroleum Exporting Countries (OPEC)

Non-Communist countries import most of the oil they need to buy abroad from the Middle East. By far the biggest oil exporter is Saudi Arabia. In 1960 the main oil-exporting countries banded together to form OPEC. Map 3 shows the present members (see also p. 104).

Many of the OPEC members are in the Middle East. These countries have become very important, for the following reasons:

1 Many countries in the world, including North America, Japan and Western Europe depend upon this oil. For example, there was a serious crisis in 1973. In that year the Arab countries stopped selling oil to some countries who were supporting Israel in its war against the Arabs. This had

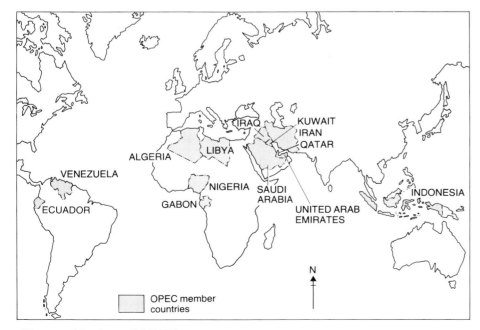

Map 3   Members of OPEC

Minerals and fuels

a serious effect especially in the United States, West Germany and Holland where petrol became scarce.

2 OPEC has been able to increase the price of oil: it is so necessary to have assured supplies that people are willing to pay higher prices. Big increases in prices were introduced in 1973 and 1979.

3 The countries with a lot of oil to sell have earned huge sums of money. Poor countries needing to import oil have become even poorer because they now must spend so much more for their oil.

4 Many people have become extremely worried about possible wars or revolutions in the Middle East that might affect oil supplies again. The USA is particularly worried about possible Russian control of the region, especially as oil will become quite scarce by the turn of the century.

Sheikh Yamani, the Saudi Arabian Minister of Petroleum and Mineral Resources, has shown great statesmanship since the mid-1970s in keeping the supply and price of oil reasonably stable

Nuclear power

Nuclear power stations and fission power

Because the world's deposits of oil are being rapidly used up, increasing attention is being given to alternative sources of energy. The most important is nuclear power.

The tremendous energy released by nuclear reactions was first used for making bombs (see pp. 14–15). But the splitting (or 'fission', see fig 2, p. 14) of atoms of uranium or plutonium as used in atomic bombs can now be controlled so that the energy is released gradually. This energy can then be used for generating electricity.

By the early 1980s about 6% of the world's electricity was produced this way. In some countries over 10% of their electricity comes from nuclear power stations – in the USA, Belgium, Sweden, West Germany. By 1983 Britain was producing about 14% of its electricity by nuclear power. There are plans to increase this considerably early in the next century (see map 4).

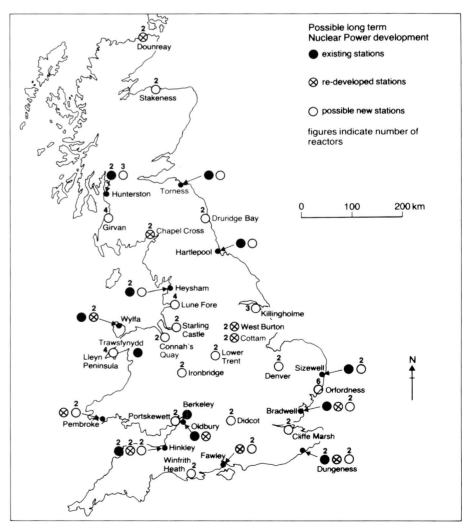

Map 4   Present and planned nuclear power stations in Britain

Minerals and fuels

Objections to nuclear power stations

The world's supply of uranium will last longer than oil. It might seem sensible therefore to replace oil-fired generators with nuclear reactors. But there are problems. The basic fuel (uranium or plutonium) is radioactive. Radiation can be extremely dangerous (see pp. 14–15); it can cause diseases like cancer; it can kill; it can deform unborn babies. Many people object to the building of nuclear power stations for the following reasons:

1 Accidents can happen at power stations. Radioactive liquid can seep out. More seriously, if safety devices fail, a power station could explode. This very nearly happened at a place called Three Mile Island in the USA in 1979.

2 Nuclear reactors produce radioactive waste. The waste can remain radioactive for a very long time – many thousands of years. This waste has to be transported safely and stored safely. Again, accidents could happen.

3 The uranium or plutonium for nuclear power stations can also be used for making nuclear weapons. Therefore countries with nuclear power stations could also secretly make bombs (see p. 14). Also, terrorists (see pp. 5–7) could steal material from a power station or while it was being transported to a power station: they could then make a bomb.

Because of these serious dangers, many people have demonstrated against nuclear power stations. Some of the protests have been quite violent, especially in the USA, Japan, France, West Germany, Switzerland and Spain.

This photograph shows one of the most serious demonstrations against nuclear power stations in recent years. The site was Kalkar in West Germany: 30 000 demonstrators (from the Netherlands and Germany) faced police. The police used tear-gas; the demonstrators wore masks for protection

Fusion power

As we saw on p. 14, there are two main kinds of nuclear weapons. One works by the splitting (or 'fission') of atoms of uranium or plutonium. And this release of energy can be controlled to produce electricity.

The other works by the joining (or 'fusion' (see fig 3, p. 14)) of atoms of hydrogen. Experiments are being made to control this release of energy too, though it is much more difficult.

In Britain the research is being undertaken at laboratories at Culham in Oxfordshire. Scientists and engineers hope that by the early years of the next century, fusion reactors will be producing electricity. Fusion reactors have two very great advantages over fission reactors:

1 Hydrogen can be obtained from water – there are therefore limitless supplies;

2 it is a much safer process.

Lime dropped into a Swedish lake to neutralize the acid

Trees in Czechoslovakia killed by acid rain

Smoke

Until quite recently large industrial cities, in certain weather conditions, would be blanketed in dense fog. This was caused by smoke from coal-fires in homes and factory chimneys. Traffic would be slowed to a halt and people with weak chests and hearts suffered serious discomfort; some died. Many cities have now made clean air zones where it is forbidden to burn anything except smokeless fuels. Industrial fog, or 'smog' as it was called, is less common.

Ozone layer

'Ozone' is a rich form of oxygen. A layer of ozone surrounds the earth, very high up. Some of the rays from the sun would be very dangerous if they reached the earth, but they are stopped by the ozone layer. The ozone layer is therefore very important. Some people believe that it is being damaged – by the exhausts of high-flying aeroplanes and by aerosols.

Acid rain

A particularly serious form of pollution today is acid rain. Acid contained in smoke, especially smoke from power stations, is carried by winds and then falls to earth again in rain. Sweden seems to be particularly affected by this form of pollution from Britain – with some horrific results:

1 Many of Sweden's lakes are 'dead', that is, all life forms have been killed.

2 Well-water is polluted.

3 Babies suffer from diarrhoea.

4 The hair of some blond people has been turned green.

Pollution

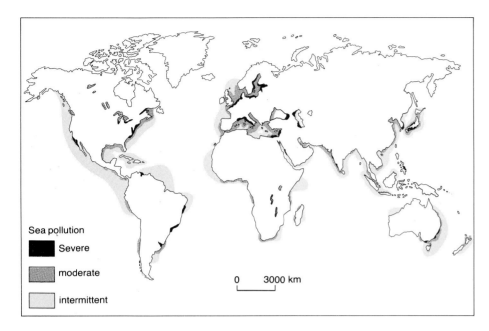

Map 5   Pollution of the world's seas. Ships sometimes pollute the sea if they are damaged in collision – for example, the spillage of oil from tankers involved in accidents. In 1984 came the first scare of radio-active pollution from this cause: a ship carrying nuclear waste was sunk in the North Sea

Sea pollution

■ Severe

▨ moderate

░ intermittent

0   3000 km

Noise

A different kind of pollution comes from noise. People living near airports suffer from the high-pitched screams of jet engines. Some jobs require people to work in conditions of loud noise. So ear-muffs must be worn to prevent permanent damage to hearing.

Water

Many laws have recently been passed to prevent people from polluting the earth's waters. But they are only gradually becoming effective. Rivers in some parts of the world are still treated as sewers, and seas as cess-pits. Factories empty their poisonous wastes into rivers; human sewage is pumped into seas; industrial waste is dumped at sea; ships discharge oil into the sea. As a result fish and sea-birds are poisoned or killed. Huge lakes near industrial towns have been killed such as Lake Erie in North America, and Lake Baikal in Siberia.

The most notorious case is probably the Mediterranean. Because the Straits of Gibraltar are so narrow, the Mediterranean Sea is almost like a large lake with no great tides to disperse the pollution. It is even quite dangerous to swim off certain coasts.

A workman wearing ear-muffs for protection against the noise of his pneumatic-drill

10.5 Possible solutions

Restrictions

As we noticed at the beginning of this chapter, the two main causes of strain on the world's eco-system are:

1 the population explosion;
2 widespread industrialization.

A number of scientists believe that the only effective way to reduce the rate of resource depletion and pollution is to tackle these two causes. This would mean more widespread birth-control and preventing the LDCs (see pp. 92 and 98) from industrializing.

To ensure that birth-control is put into practice, governments have tried to impose it, as in India and especially in China. But birth-control seems to threaten the rights of individuals to decide how many children they will have. To stop industrialization in countries like Asia, Africa and South America seems very unfair because they would be prevented from raising their standards of living.

'Small is beautiful'

Some people believe that generally increasing size is the basic problem. Cities have become bigger; industrial and commercial firms have become larger; and, especially in the rich countries, we are generally greedy for more – more cars, more foreign holidays, etc. A famous writer, E F Schumacher, coined the phrase 'small is beautiful' to try to persuade people that these trends are dangerous and must be reversed.

Increasing resources

There are a number of ways of making the best use of the earth's resources or of using new sources (see pp. 140 and 142). This can be done by:

1 recycling used materials;
2 substituting materials;
3 producing energy from the development of alternative technology;
4 mining the sea-bed and, eventually, other planets.

Actions by voluntary and government bodies

Voluntary bodies

People are becoming increasingly conscious of ecological problems. In many countries voluntary bodies have been created either for conservation work or to put pressure upon governments to take a more responsible attitude.

In Britain for example there are a very large number of conservation societies, such as the 'Wildfowl Trust', or 'Keep Britain Tidy'. Some voluntary organizations are international, such as 'Friends of the Earth', and 'Greenpeace' (who are campaigning to save the whale from extinction). In West Germany, environmentalists have even formed an important political party, called the 'Green Party'. There is also a Green Party in Britain.

Government action

Governments themselves have also taken action. For example: Clean Air Acts in Britain; laws against killing elephants for ivory in East Africa; speed restrictions in the USA to save petrol.

International action

Governments of several countries are meeting increasingly to deal with environmental problems. For example, the countries with Mediterranean coastlines are combining efforts to clean up the pollution there.

In 1972 the United Nations organized a Conference on the Human Environment in Stockholm. As a result, a permanent UN organization was set up called UNEP (United Nations Environment Programme). It has its offices in Nairobi (Kenya). It investigates problems and warns and advises about the damage mankind is causing on planet Earth.

The campaign in Britain to prevent litter

Questions

1. a What is the 'eco-system'? What is 'ecology'?
   b List the six main ways in which the eco-system is being endangered.
   c List four ways in which food production can be increased. What are the problems?
   d What are 'fossil fuels'?
   e What do the following initials mean? (i) OPEC; (ii) UNEP; (iii) DDT.
   f Find out from someone who has a car and who uses it for travelling to work what proportion of the weekly income is spent on petrol and what proportion is spent on food.
   g What are the three main objections to nuclear power stations?
   h Why are many of Sweden's lakes dying?
   i Explain briefly why the population explosion and industrialization are such serious problems.
   j What is the name of the environmental political party in West Germany?

2. Write an essay or hold a class discussion on whether Britain should build any more nuclear power stations.

3. Write a report on the work of a local conservation society.

4. Read the following extract and answer the questions.

   ❛ At present and projected growth rates, the world's population would reach 10 billion by 2030 and would approach 30 billion by the end of the twenty-first century. These levels correspond closely to estimates by the US National Academy of Sciences of the maximum carrying capacity of the entire earth. Already the populations in sub-Saharan Africa and in the Himalayan hills of Asia have exceeded the carrying capacity of the immediate area, triggering an erosion of the land's capacity to support life. The resulting poverty and ill health have further complicated efforts to reduce fertility. Unless this circle of interlinked problems is broken soon, population growth in such areas will unfortunately be slowed for reasons other than declining birth rates. Hunger and disease will claim more babies and young children, and more of those surviving will be mentally and physically handicapped by childhood malnutrition.

   Indeed, the problems of preserving the carrying capacity of the earth and sustaining the possibility of a decent life for the human beings that inhabit it are enormous and close upon us. Yet there is reason for hope. It must be emphasized that the Global 2000 Study's projections are based on the assumption that national policies regarding population

stabilization, resource conservation, and environmental protection will remain essentially unchanged through the end of the century. But in fact, policies are beginning to change. In some areas, forests are being replanted after cutting. Some nations are taking steps to reduce soil losses and desertification. Interest in energy conservation is growing, and large sums are being invested in exploring alternatives to petroleum dependence. The need for family planning is slowly becoming better understood. Water supplies are being improved and waste treatment systems built. High-yield seeds are widely available and seed banks are being expanded. Some wildlands with their genetic resources are being protected. Natural predators and selective pesticides are being substituted for persistent and destructive pesticides. ❜

(From a report written for President Carter, 1981.)

   a Draw a graph showing the projected increase in world population from 1984 (see fig 2, p. 101), 2000 (see map 8, p. 107), 2030 and 2100.
   b List the arguments in the extract: (i) for pessimism and (ii) for optimism about the future of the world.
   c What single change do you think would have the most beneficial effect on the condition of the world? Give your reasons.

5. Look at the table below and answer the questions.

Estimates of World Forest Resources, 1978 and 2000	Closed Forest* (millions of hectares)	
	1978	2000
USSR	785	775
Europe	140	150
North America	470	464
Japan, Australia, New Zealand	69	68
Subtotal	1457	14645
Latin America	550	329
Africa	188	150
Asia and Pacific LDCs	361	181
Subtotal (LDCs)	1099	660
Total (world)	2563	2117

*'Closed Forest' is a dense and productive forest

Fig 2   The problem of deforestation

   a Which main region of the world is likely to lose the largest: (i) *area* of forest by the end of the century; (ii) *percentage* of its forest area by the end of the century?
   b Which main region of the world is likely to increase its area of forest by the end of the century?
   c What percentage of the world's forest is likely to be lost by the end of the century?

Index

Index

Acknowledgements

The publishers would like to thank the following for permission to reproduce photographic material:

Christer Ågren: p. 144 (*left*); Amena Picture Library: p. 69 (*bottom*); Associated Press Ltd: p. 71; Barnaby's Picture Library: pp. 92 (*right*), 139; BBC Hulton Picture Library: pp. 30 (*top*), 77 (bottom *left*); British Museum: p. 30 (*centre*); British Telecommunications plc: p. 127; Camerapix/Hutchison Library: pp. 77 (*top left and right, bottom right*), 137; Camera Press Ltd: pp. 22 (*top*), 23 (*bottom*), 33 (*bottom*), 68 (*top*); Earthscan/Mark Edwards: pp. 92 (*left*), 93, 99 (*top*); Diana East: p. 94 (*bottom*); Eastern European Bible Mission: p. 60 (*top*), FBC Ltd: p. 138; Ferranti Electronics Ltd: p. 131 (*top*); Ford Motor Company: p. 132; The Guardian: p. 29; David Hoffman: p. 79 (*top*); Imperial War Museum: p. 30 (*bottom*); International Defence and Aid Fund: p. 90; International Planned Parenthood Federation: p. 105 (*left*); Keep Britain Tidy Group: p. 146; Mansell Collection Ltd: p. 74 (*bottom*); Mary Evans Picture Library: p. 74 (*top*); National Economic Development Council: p. 118 (*top*); National Film Archive, London: p. 130; Novosti Press: p. 50; The Observer: p. 60; Oxfam: pp. 99 (*bottom*), 106; Pacemaker Press, Belfast: p. 5; The Photo Source: pp. 2, 6, 8, 9, 13, 15, 16 (*top*), 17 (*bottom*), 26 (*bottom*), 32 (*top*), 33 (*top*), 49 (*bottom*), 51 (*bottom*), 52, 63, 64, 69 (*top*), 81, 85, 86, 87, 104; Popperfoto: pp. 31, 32 (*bottom*), 37, 51 (*top*), 57 (*bottom*), 62, 66, 75, 83, 84 (*top*), 89 (*top*), 100, 119, 126, 142; Punch: pp. 46, 62, 80; Racal Safety Ltd: p. 145; Rex Features Ltd: pp. 7, 22 (*bottom*), 25, 72, 144 (*right*); S & G Press Agency Ltd: p. 26 (*top*); Gerald Scarfe: p. 67; Spectrum Colour Library: p. 125; Frank Spooner Pictures: pp. 17 (*top*), 33 (*bottom*), 53, 68 (*bottom*), 70; Topham Picture Library: pp. 3, 11, 16 (*bottom*), 23 (*top*), 27, 48, 49 (*top*), 54, 57 (*top*), 65, 73, 84 (*bottom*), 89 (*bottom*), 124, 129, 131 (*bottom*), 133, 143; U.P.I: p. 30 (*centre*); UK Committee for UNICEF: p. 44 (*bottom*); United Nations Information Centre: pp. 18, 34, 35, 36, 38, 39, 41, 42, 44 (*top*), 45, 95, 102, 116; The Wiener Library: p. 79; The World Bank: p. 113.

Map 6 p. 72 after M Gilbert; Map 1 p. 93 after A Boyd; Fig 1 p. 110 after Pan New State of the World Atlas, 1984; Map 3 p. 128 after B J L Berry.

The estate of the late Sonia Brownwell Orwell and Martin Secker and Warburg Ltd: poem p. 61.

Every effort has been made to trace copyright holders but in one or two cases without success. If anyone claiming copyright of material published but not acknowledged will contact the publishers corrections will be made in future editions.

The cartoons are by Barry Rowe.

The maps and diagrams are by Gecko Ltd.

The cover cartoon is by Kal